BRITANNIA MILL

Discard

01.

D1143416

PHOTO-GRAPHIC

VISION

BRITANNIA MILL

An artist's eye

scrutiny

is like

the gentle touch

of a blind

man's hands

over the sad face

of a young girl.

No purpose

but to know.

to Myrta, my wife, who bore with me—and Gordon, Julian, and Vivian, my children, who couldn't but . . .

PHOTO-GRAPHIC

VISION

by ZVONKO GLYCK

AMPHOTO

American Photographic Book Publishing Co., Inc.

NEW YORK

COPYRIGHT © 1965 BY ZVONKO GLYCK

Published in New York by Amphoto, and simultaneously
in Toronto, Canada, by Ambassador Books, Ltd.
All rights reserved. No part of this book may be
reproduced in any form without the written
consent of the publisher.

LIBRARY OF CONGRESS CATALOG CARD NO 65-23147

PRINTED IN THE UNITED STATES OF AMERICA

770·11

DERBY & DISTRICT
O. NO.   1 0 NOV 1967 £5·12s·0d
163788
COL   OF ART

34·7060

For permission to use photographs
which they published previously, I
should like to thank the following
Newsweek magazine, for the photograph on page 81; *Esquire* magazine, for
the photographs of Scott Fitzgerald on
page 144 from the black and white
original on page 145 supplied by
them; Time-Life Books, for the
photographs on pages 140-41; *Popular
Photography,* for the pictures on
pages 129 and 152.

I wish to express my gratitude to the
publisher and staff of Amphoto, who
made this book possible and who
collaborated so willingly and diligently
on the completion of it.

CREDITS

Designer: *Herbert M. Rosenthal*
Printing, Color: *Davis Delaney, Inc., New York, N. Y.*
Printing, Black & White: *Halliday Lithograph, West Hanover, Mass.*
Linecolor separations: *Zvonko Glyck*
Binding: *Sendor Bindery, New York, N. Y.*
Paper, Color: *Prentice Enamel Dull, West Virginia Pulp and Paper Company*
Paper, Black and White: *Navaho Opaque, Baldwin Paper Company*
Cover: *Columbia Mills' Vynside*
Dies: *Alcon Engraving*
Endpapers: *Multicolor Endleaf, Lindenmeyr Schlosser Company*

*The type for this book was set by York Typesetting Company
of New York City. The body copy is set in 10/13 Optima, the chapter
titles and initial letters in Palatino Semibold, and the folios in Optima.
Optima, with its Italic and Semibold variants, is also employed in
the miscellaneous material in the frontmatter and glossary. The
title of the book is in Palatino Semibold. The photograph numbers
are in Helvetica.*

FOREWORD

Photographic Vision is a book an editor dreams about, one
that allows him to enter into creative concert with author,
designer, typographer, and printer to build a work of art into
a harmonious whole from inception of idea to delivery
of bound and jacketed books.

It is a fascinating though often frustrating experience. It is a
task that requires seemingly endless conferences, eye-straining
sorting of hundreds of exciting pictures, laying out of pages
that coordinate text and pictures and remain visually attractive,
editing and re-editing a dense text, and making further
changes and corrections in galley proofs, page proofs, and
repros. It is a task that sees tempers strained, egos bruised, and
deadlines stretched. Nevertheless, none of the many persons
involved would have given up the opportunity to participate,
and all will have a shared sense of pride in the result.

Not the least difficult, but most thoroughly enjoyable, part
of the job is working with the author. Zvonko Glyck is
the most truly protean man I have ever known. His is a keenly
intelligent mind in constant operation, an artistically sensitive
emotion in steady excitement, a volatile complex of
creativity that never ceases to function.

The results have been most gratifying, for we have here a
book that is healthy, invigorating, and clear-sighted. Take away
the title and the illustrations and we still have a commentary
of utmost relevance to any endeavor requiring creative
conceptual freedom.

This foreword hints at the number of people involved
in the publication of *Photographic Vision,* and the last page
of the book gives proper credit to many of them. But it is
Zvonko Glyck's name that appears on the title page, and
that is how it should be, for the vision is his, and so is the book.

LESTER KAPLAN
Editor-in-Chief, Amphoto

It is in the nature of man

to comprehend first

things he respects.

He accepts them with a bow,

then harbors them,

and finally

defends them fanatically.

Only when he starts

to wonder

about the origin of his respect

is the process of thinking generated,

reasoning started,

and the holocaust of creativity

begins to take its toll.

2

13

CONCEPT

1

3

Anybody concerned with communicating visually through photography is faced at some time with the apparent limitations inherent in the medium. The purpose of this book is constructively disputing the existence of most of these limitations. It is an essay on the inducement and amplification of Photographic Vision.

In preparing the book, I became aware of a desire to define my audience. Was I talking to the photographer, the art director, the artist, the painter, the editor, the copywriter? The desire to share my experience and to communicate my views and ideas was so intense that I decided not to specify or limit my audience. I hope that the reader will not only be induced to explore the application of the techniques displayed, but will be dynamically stimulated by his reactions to the opinions and attitudes in these pages. Should portions of the text appear too basic, the initiated will understand that they are meant as background information for the less cognizant.

When I address myself to the photographer, I shall not make any distinction between the professional and non-professional. It is not relevant whether he (or she) has committed himself to a creative project on his own initiative or has been assigned to it by someone else. The non-professional, or amateur, is responsible to himself alone for the results he produces, and he can apply himself whenever he chooses to. The professional is an amateur who has developed a faster and more practiced triggering of his creative assembly. He has accepted the challenge of producing results that will be subject to judgment by somebody else—all within the framework of editorial and production requirements and deadlines. The professional has chosen not to look for easy excuses by considering this as interference with his integrity. He has organized his mind and activated the metamorphosis from "having to" into "wanting to." He therefore remains an amateur in the original and best sense of the word: lover of, who is in love, who has passion for what he is doing. When the word is used in this book, it shall always be in this sense, and not with any implication of beginner, fumbler, or with any hint of incompetence, or any attitude that gives a make-believe status to a person who does not ask for it in the first place.

4

5

Mostly I will be addressing those who, for various reasons, hesitate to consider themselves artists, who have been hypnotized into an inability to apply the main part of their creative talent because of the stultifying influence of fossilized, obsolete opinions. Their docile acceptance of the "average mind" status is my concern. Average mind, average talent, average man— all of which implies a lower-grade classification not seriously to be considered except for purposes of exploitation. Today, children are considered to be creative. Their work is believed to contain elements of art in the purest sense. Isn't it amazing that the authorities who have decided upon the innate creativity of children are the very same who ignore the existence of these creative powers in most adults? How do we account for this? The child releases his creative powers without effort or awareness. The adult, having gone through a long schooling, has been convinced that he has no justification for exercising his talent, unless he displays especially strong manifestations of creative talent. This may be no more than the ability of the individual to remain unimpressed by the learned denial of his creativeness. Creative potential is imbedded in everybody. The license to practice this quality is granted either by education, surroundings, or the unrelenting urge that disregards obstacles. The absence of this urge is not equivalent to a lack of creative ability, for this ability can be induced and cultivated.

Different means have been devised to curb creativeness in the "average'" man: obedience, respect, schedules, intimidation, scorn, inflating of apparent values, emphasis on false values, glorification of humdrum, mass production, false authorities, standard-setting organizations and publications, intellectual aristocracy, cliques, groups, etc., etc., etc. All of this accompanied by the roar of the motif: "The privileges of the mind are for but a few."

Traditional misconceptions, with their resulting prejudices and caste-creating properties, are too often accepted as sane authorities. They are not. Proverbs, axioms, quotations, and similar wisecracks are presented as universal truths of unquestionable value, especially when projected in impressive rhetorical tones or published in "authoritative" books. All of this tends to perpetuate the status quo of human thought of hundreds, even thousands, of years ago. Since we are fed these wisdoms from our birth, the conclusions we draw from them acquire almost atavistic importance, regardless of their irrationality. Thus, the poet or artist is supposed to be an eccentric, a bohemian, unable to cope realistically with the vicissitudes of everyday life. He accepts this concept and strives to live up to it in all respects, even to the extent of colonizing with others like himself. He is credited with a certain amount of promiscuity, while at the same time his masculinity and virility are questioned. He is an enviable and somewhat glamorous oddity, but definitely inadequate. His true, universal contribution is shrugged off. All of which results in the reluctance of the "average," "normal" individual to recognize, accept, and explore his own poetic or artistic potential. In this evidently mental process, the awareness of its components could justify the liberation of the mind from the rut of conventional thinking habits. A perfectly normal paterfamilias could suddenly find himself faced with the joy and threat of the questions: "How do I look at something? How do I see it? Should I communicate it to the universe?"

It is no small achievement to extricate oneself from this rut. One may find himself in it through negligence, ignorance, or external pressure. The promotion of mediocrity is an old feudal and aristocratic device, and it still plagues us—in a different form, perhaps, but it is here. Liberation from these influences is, at this time, the task of the individual. No real rebellion or anarchy is involved, merely the realization of one's true abilities. This realization can only evolve from experience and intense self-education, otherwise it could very well degenerate into narcissistic self-admiration without ever getting close to the objectivity of the original intention. The search for the potential, as it progresses, becomes the result.

One should be able to apply a major part of his creative abilities, regardless of the amount of inhibiting browbeating he has suffered. He should be able to permit himself to create new means, new devices, new tools, whenever he needs them to elaborate on an idea. Even if these do not serve an immediate purpose and are only partially satisfying, the effort of exploring and creating is worth while. It is necessary, in the interest of the progress of photography as a medium of serious art, to reevaluate all preconceived notions and rules that are supposed to govern the basic quality standards of the photographic image. These rules may be disregarded only after one is adequately familiar with them. After one has managed to judge them as opinions and considerations, valid at the time they were made, their "anecdotic value" as components of the history of photography will become obvious. But it is destructive, in terms of progress, to hide behind standards and rules, to avoid or suppress the labor of free experimentation, with all its inherent unpredictability, disappointments, and surprises. As in the other arts, in photography the final product can often be no more than a phase of experimentation.

Once the license to be creative has been granted, or appropriated, a giant step toward the acquisition of photographic vision has been made, for photographic vision is an acquired attitude—the ability to see in terms of the finished photograph. It is the ability to see selectively and to feel what the image will be like when any of the photographic means at the photog-

13

rapher's command is applied. Whether this is done before, during, or after the initial exposure is relevant only to purpose or subject. It is the power of visually choosing the important and valid, the symbolic and subtle, the realistic and crude. This can be practiced with or without a camera, though it is sometimes difficult to visualize without the aid of the ground glass of the camera because of the limitations and accommodations of the eye-mind mechanism. The ground glass of the camera is an essential instrument of photographic vision. But only that of the single-lens reflex, press, or view camera; not that of the twin-lens reflex, since the viewing lens of the twin-lens reflex has no aperture control, and changes in aperture made in the taking lens cannot be observed. In other words, the ground glass of the camera will let us enter into a relationship with elements the eye will refuse to communicate. By throwing elements into or out of focus (through changes in the distance focused upon and the aperture setting of the lens), the interplay of elements is tampered with. When photographic vision relates to perception through imagination, it becomes obvious that this imagination can be generated only in relation to past experience. Only by conquering the technical elements of photography, or that part of it one is willing to limit himself to, can this be accomplished. It is impossible to relate something to past experience if there is none or too little. It goes without saying that an acquaintance with the work of other artists is imperative, if for no other reason than to amplify criteria and judgments. Experimentation that will result in a provoked accident, or that has an intended direction, is also part of photographic vision. Here again the outcome will depend greatly on previous experimentation and the knowledge thus acquired. Photographic vision is not the result of a recipe, but of hard and serious work by the photographer or critic.

There is no comparison or competition between prose and poetry, between free verse and rhyme, fiction or non-fiction, or between any divergent works of literature. In the same way there is no necessity of comparison or implied competition between the different creative applications of photography, their techniques and manipulations. There is no limit to the eloquence of photography. The ability of photography to record is but one of an immense number of possibilities.

The fact that a photographic record can communicate directly or evoke response by immediate projection is as basic to the art as the skeletal structure of a factory to its eventual function. To accept this skeleton as a final result implies some limitations in one's mental processes. Yet, in the judgment of today's upper levels of photographic "propriety," this perpetuation of photographic illiteracy is prevalent, inhibiting progress with senile obstinacy. These judges will, in defense of their appointed or acquired positions, stand safely shielded behind photographic standards established decades ago. To be progressive would be, in their opinion, to bring their position into jeopardy. The pioneering, for them, has been done by Daguerre or someone around there. Photojournalism is an aspect of photography of monumental importance, but still it is a small part and not all of photography.

Those who are, for some reason or accident, called upon to impress the public with their opinions should learn to evaluate the subtler interpretative and creative aspects of photography. They should learn to get over the original mystery of photography and explore other mysteries, inherent but not quite as obvious. They should stop glorifying the past, put it into history, and start appreciating, if not glorifying, the present. They should train themselves out of the habit of shrugging off unphotographic photography. They should learn to understand, instead of thundering monotonous, stereotyped, obsolete, philistine psuedo-truths. Again and again, they should be made aware that behind any photographic image, behind any unphotographic photographic image, there is a mind—not just a well-trained eye and a shutter-pressing finger—a mind that is to be considered seriously for its universal value, for its creative potential, its latent ability for expression. The searching for truth, the seeking in photography, goes far beyond the emotional jolt produced by the record of the unavoidable pain on the face of a child-bearing mother, or the placid, grandiose rocky landscape perfectly in focus. The palette of the photographer has much more than that on it. That should be kept in mind by whoever passes judgment on photography.

PAGE 23

MATERIALS
2

17

Every photographic material manufactured undergoes an unbelieveably intricate scientific scrutiny, with the emphasis on eliminating from it every element that could be considered a variable or an unknown. When such a material is released for consumption, its predictability, purpose, and usage is clearly defined by the manufacturer in an accompanying pamphlet or a brochure obtainable on request. For this, as a rule, the manufacturer takes full responsibility. If, however, you decide to digress from the uses intended for the material, you are on your own and have to write your own pamphlet.

You may be intrigued by the properties of a material that you feel you would like to apply creatively, only to find that the processing, as described in the accompanying instruction sheet, requires special equipment and intricate procedures that seem rather discouraging at first. If such is the case, you should, with a little research and ingenuity, be able to adapt the elements called for in the instruction sheet to your own conditions. By analyzing the prohibitive cost elements in the instructions and the basic uses to which they are put, you will, in all probability, find something that will substitute beautifully. Let us assume that a high intensity arc light is called for. You can use a flood light or a black light fluorescent tube instead. Such a substitution will, of course, call for compensating exposure with time and distance, which should be established by experiment. Consequently, you may find yourself exposing for seven minutes instead of ten seconds. So what? I'm sure you can find something to do during the exposure. If a vacuum printing frame is called for, your regular contact printing frame should be adequate. If ammonia vapor development with some elaborate equipment is called for, a one gallon jar filled with household ammonia will serve. Any inventiveness you apply in solving technical problems will prove to be an excellent exercise in resourcefulness. This, in turn, could justify the propelling of your ingenuity into action when more complex challenges are to be met.

There are other conditions that tend to dissuade you from getting involved in experimentation with certain materials. One is the fact that some materials are marketed in packages too large for what you think your needs are or your budget can bear. In addition, special developers may be called for, such as the two-solution developer (each a gallon) necessary for some lithographic materials. In order to get acquainted with a material, you will, as a rule, need a greater quantity than the optimism of your initial enthusiasm would suggest. It is most annoying to find yourself running out of essential material in the middle of an experiment. Furthermore, you will be more liberal in your experimentation and induced to go further, when the peril of running short of material is minimized. The end of a package of material can sometimes mean abandoning a search, when such an interruption could be welcome because of some discouraging step in the procedure. Such a wasteful ending is a discouraging experience, resulting in the arrogant self-justification of superficial knowledge. It is therefore advisable that you run the risk of remaining with a few unused sheets in the package.

The unorthodox use of materials intended for specific purposes would probably shock the manufacturer, but will enrich you with elements of discovery that you will know are your own. Even if you do not find immediate application for the results of your experiment, you will have become intimate with the medium beyond the limits that any written text can offer. It seems almost blasphemous to tamper with the properties of a material whose characteristics have been defined by the most elaborate and precise sensitometric methods. The defiance of such tampering is justified by the creative motives of the procedure.

Let us take, for instance, the Sabattier effect, or solarization —a process founded on the tendency of a photosensitive emulsion partially or totally to reverse in terms of positive-negative, if exposed for a short time during development to a light to which the emulsion is sensitive. The results will differ depending on the intensity of the light, distance from the light to the negative or print, the nature and age of the developer, the stage of the development at which the exposure to the light is made, and other variables that might become evident in a variety of experiments. Therefore, it would be misleading to give a recipe for the procedure, which would imply predictability.

In this outline of the basic steps in the process, let me emphasize that no accuracy is implied, but only an approximate illustration of the values mentioned. Let us assume that you have established the exposure necessary to produce a satisfactory enlargement on #3 paper. (Do not use variable contrast paper.) With your usual developer, development is one and a half minutes. The white light overhead is strong enough to allow you to read small print at the level of the tray.

Make your enlargement on a fresh sheet of paper. Put the paper in the developer tray, and after turning it over rapidly several times, press it to the bottom with the emulsion side up. Keeping one hand on the light switch, observe the print until you see a faint but distinct image appear. Then turn on the overhead lights for one or two seconds. After this, the image is going to darken all over. At the point before the original is completely obscured, pull the print out and submerge it in

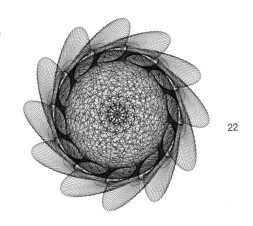

22

the stop bath, which should stop development immediately. After that, fix in the usual manner. The result may appear quite disappointing when viewed by reflected light; however, if viewed as a transparency, with a light behind the print, the result will be more encouraging. After having washed and dried this solarized print, make a contact print of it in a printing frame by exposing under the enlarger light and developing normally. If all goes well, you will rejoice in the result. Should this not be the case, it means you must start from the beginning, taking all the variables into consideration: shorter or longer exposure, exposing when the image in the developing print is fainter or darker, shorter or longer print development after the second exposure. By this time, you will have acquired sufficient judgment of the variables to exercise more precise control over the finished product. You must

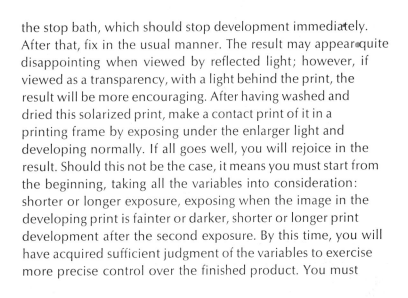

21

remember, though, that those variables continue to operate and intefere, however slightly, with the predictability you are trying to establish. Once you have produced an acceptable result, you can resolarize it, add or subtract tone, and apply all your printing knowledge towards producing variations.

When you decide to use film instead of paper, there are some pertinent factors to keep in mind. The film should be orthochromatic, or any other material that can be handled under a safelight bright enough for you to observe changes in it during development. A slow emulsion is advisable. High or normal contrast materials may be used; you will make your choice on the basis of experience or intuition. Litho materials are usable, but are rather capricious. Keep to your usual paper developer, regardless of the manufacturer's instructions for its intended use, but dilute it if the image appears too quickly.

In your arbitrary manipulation of materials, you will notice that some are more manageable than others. Some will cooperate and even contribute something unexpected; others will resist. Some are tame; others are wild. This characteristic is often connected with exposure latitude. The greater the latitude, the tamer the material, as a rule. I would consider films such as Kodak's Fine Grain Positive tame. They can be handled like enlarging paper under a bright safelight and can be used for continuous tone or line. They also respond favorably to a great variety of developers and are indispensable where a continuous tone sandwich is called for. Litho films (Kodalith, Reprolith, Photolith, etc.) are rather on the wild side and stubborn, which may be an asset, considering the uses to which you will put them.

Outdated materials have a charm of their own, not the least of which is their completely unpredictable properties. This unpredictability can be taken advantage of to provoke many unexpected but pleasing accidents, which you should treasure, for they are one-time affairs that cannot be duplicated by using any other material. Some effects in color photography can be achieved only with outdated film. The sad part of all this, however, is that as soon as you have learned something about the characteristics of the material, you are out of it. In outdated color roll film there is a certain amount of predictability as far as shift of color, contrast, and overall color cast is concerned, allowing a greater freedom of experimentation and application.

Among color films, I would consider the Kodachrome type of film wild and unmanageable in terms of unorthodox usage, and the higher speed Ektachrome type tame and manageable. At a certain point of over- or underexposure, the Kodachrome type will simply refuse to cooperate. Polacolor, with its peculiar "Old Master" color quality, is also in the category of the wild ones and can be handled only on its own terms.

Other materials useful in the development and practice of photographic vision may be found outside photographic supply stores. They are available on the shelves of grocery stores, at antiques dealers, in glass and mirror shops, five and dime stores, or among discarded items in basements and attics. It only takes a free-flowing imagination and courageous experimentation to discover and apply them to your work.

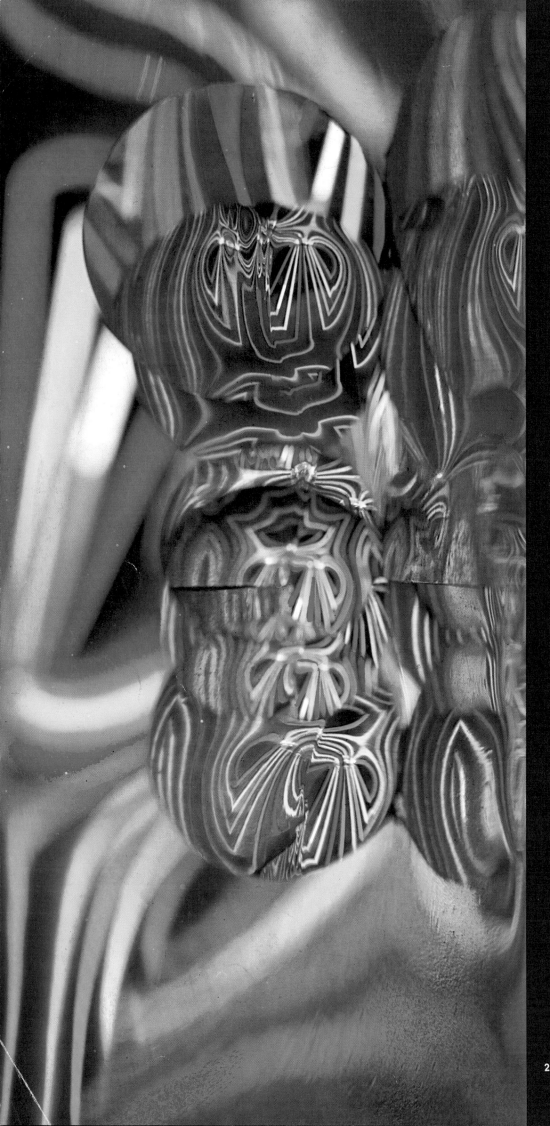

5

4   6

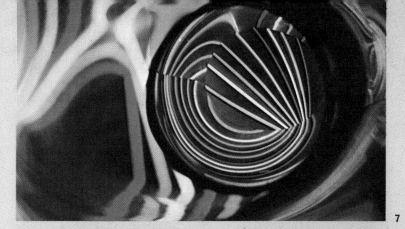

7

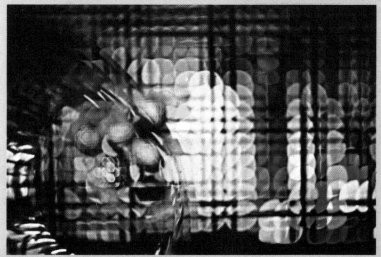

8

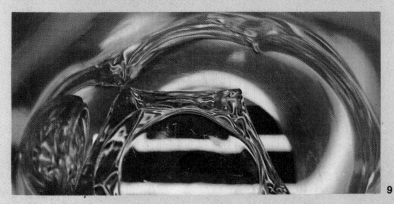

9

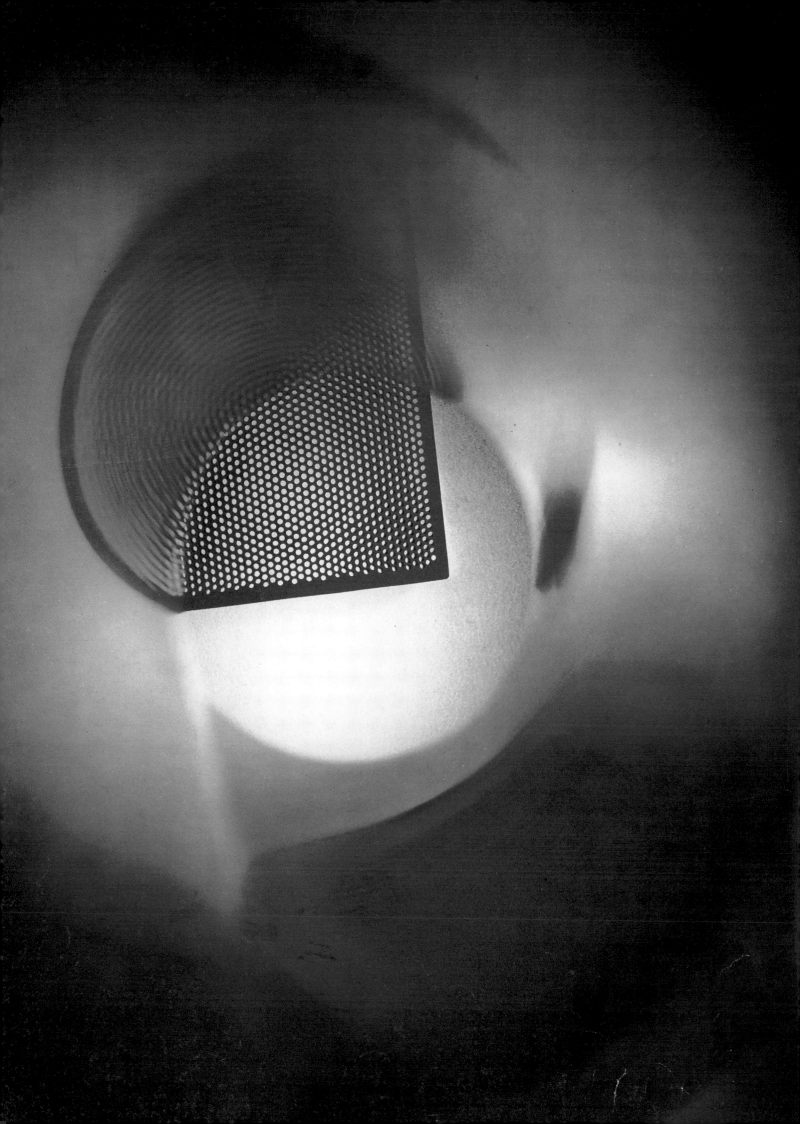

23

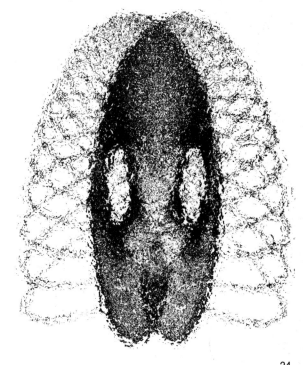

24

DESIGN
3

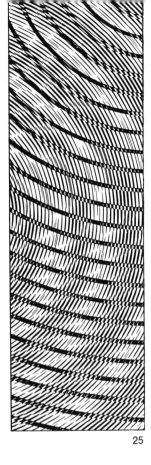

25

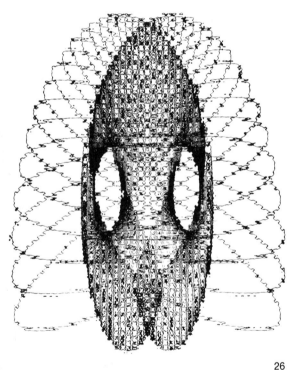

26

To get involved in created photographic design is, at first, a traumatic experience, not far short of catastrophic. Yet in spite of this, once started, one keeps on going deeper and deeper, as if drawn by the song of the sirens. The immense variety, the possibilities, the unending number of combinations, the unexpected, and then the constant agony of choice. There is no saturation point. The creative joy that accompanies all this is an experience of exaltation beyond description. One has to go through it to understand it. Fortunately, created photographic design has no imposed limitations in method or tools. Being mostly unphotographic in appearance, and often lacking in visual clues, it puzzles the alleged photographic purist and leaves him at a loss as to what to be dogmatic about. Not being really on intimate terms with photography but for a few routine processes, he has not managed to establish rules of what is permitted and what is forbidden in created photographic design. So the photographic practitioner is left free to originate without having to suffer pangs of conscience for having broken some traditional rules. Consequently, anything goes—with the camera or without it; with the enlarger or without it; via photo-chemical interaction of anything that could be remotely or scientifically considered photographic; whether intended or accidental. Only the result matters.

From the painful design of straps left on the skin of the sunbather who fell asleep under the scorching sun to the recording of a swinging light that follows the rules of gravity and the earth's rotation, we get photographic design. Extricated design, that is design extracted from a representational whole, has a charm and value of its own. The pleasure of the search and the excitement of discovery are rewards in themselves, even discounting the fact that an original has been brought into existence. Extricating design allows only a narrow latitude of manipulation because of the danger of destroying something that is an original in itself. This is in contrast to created design, where the original is arbitrary and recognizable only to the originator. It is true that in extricated design the visual clue becomes of secondary or minimal importance. Nevertheless, it plays a part, as it stimulates a different and additional range of responses than the design would if deprived

of it. A photograph of a cross-section of an artichoke is a design. If this photograph is rendered in line (high-contrast), it somehow becomes even more of a design. Recognition of the artichoke will become secondary—the resulting design is what we are involved with and respond to or enjoy. The contradiction of the simplicity and complexity of the design is what intrigues and stimulates us. Yet the underlying forces of nature are felt in the dynamic organization of the design, and we are back to the artichoke. An extricated design could very well be used in making a created design; but in the process it is advisable to eliminate recognizable clues, in order to avoid the distraction resulting from the absurdity of something being there inducing recognition of something that isn't. An independent representational unit, or several, can be incorporated into a created design without interference. As a matter of fact it could be contributory to the overall result, or could emphasize the symbolic or allegoric expression. The making of a design can be approached for its suggestive, symbolic value; for its decorative ornamental value. These values are almost always interchangeable, and will depend upon the emphasis of usage and placement.

Some seven years ago I was assigned by *Newsweek* magazine to make a symoblic photographic design for a cover story entitled "The Science of Dreams." I was delighted. Finally, an assignment that accepted the amplification of photographic means. The direction along which the assignment was to be developed referred vaguely to some designs in my portfolio. Elements that should be incorporated were suggested and a black and white solution considered.

I complied with the requirements of the art director to his greatest satisfaction. However, when I presented him with the solution he expected, I asked whether the deadline would permit a little more experimentation on my part. It is most desirable that the photographer collaborate fully and contribute more than is expected, but volunteering is not always the best policy. It might be considered meddlesome, pushy, and confusing. I was so excited over the possibility of exposing some aspects of my experimentation—and a different facet of photography—that I disregarded considerations that I would otherwise evaluate more carefully. I proceeded to conceive the result in line-color and simplified the elements included. The original concept was too busy for this version. As it turned out, this final experiment in line-color was accepted for use on the cover.

Frankly, I hoped that this unorthodox symbolic photographic solution of a visual problem would have some effect on the field of photography. Presumptuous? Yes, I agree. But then, every hope is. Sadly, no noticeable visual photographic revolution took place. Some six years later however, I had to see the same concept manifest itself in a new, well-publicized art form called Op or Retinal Art. No credit was given to photography, in spite of the obviously photographic origin of a great deal of the works displayed. I am all for crossing borders, but what irritates me is not admitting the crossing of borders into photography, as if photography were a lesser member of the fine arts.

PAGE 45

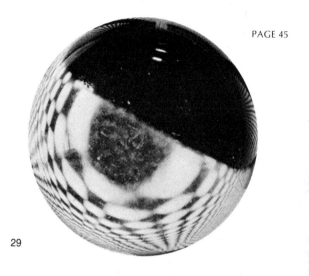

29

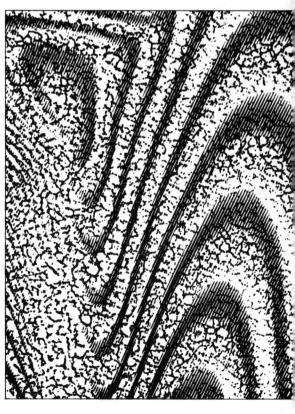

30

31

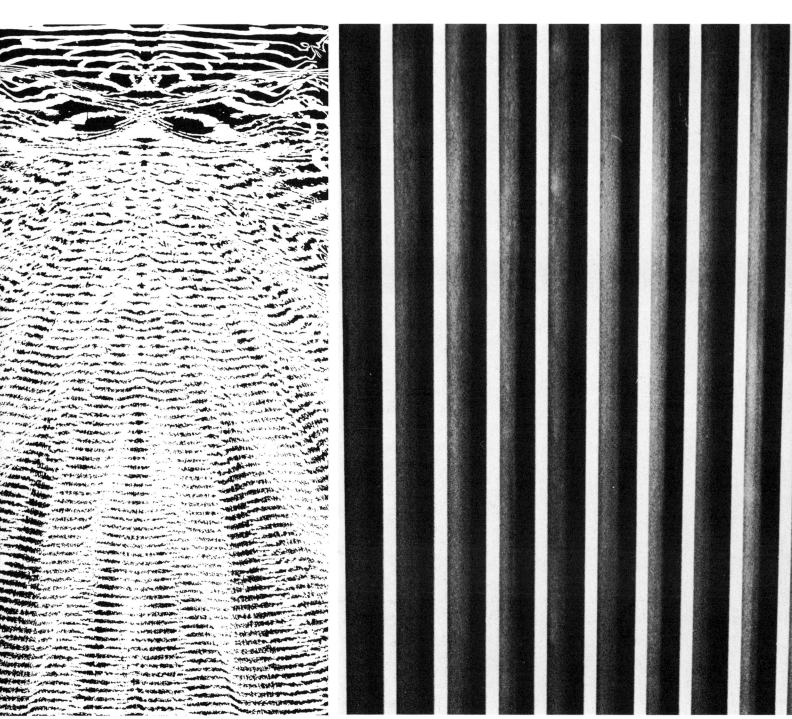

32

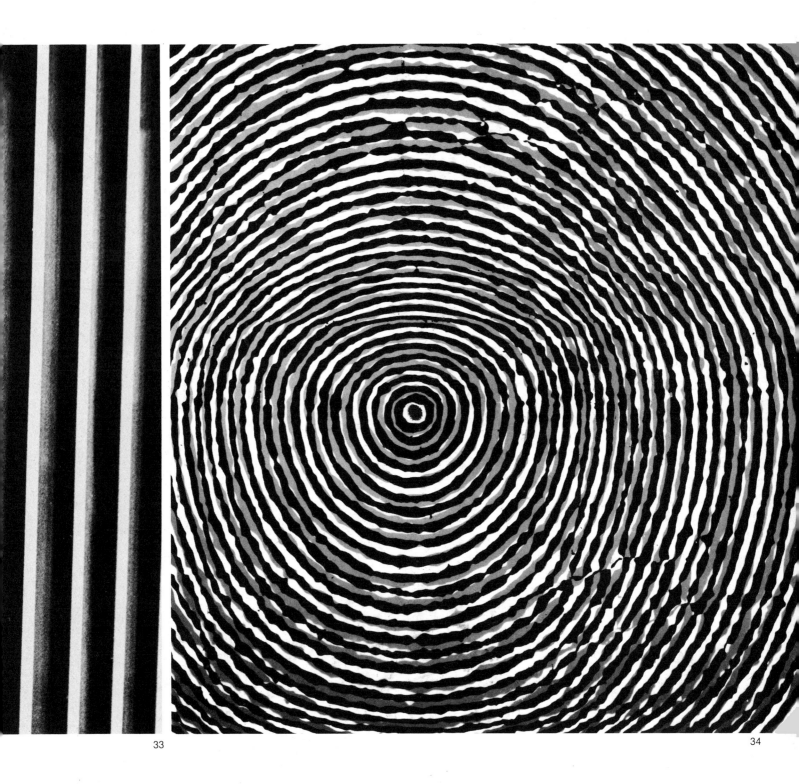

33

34

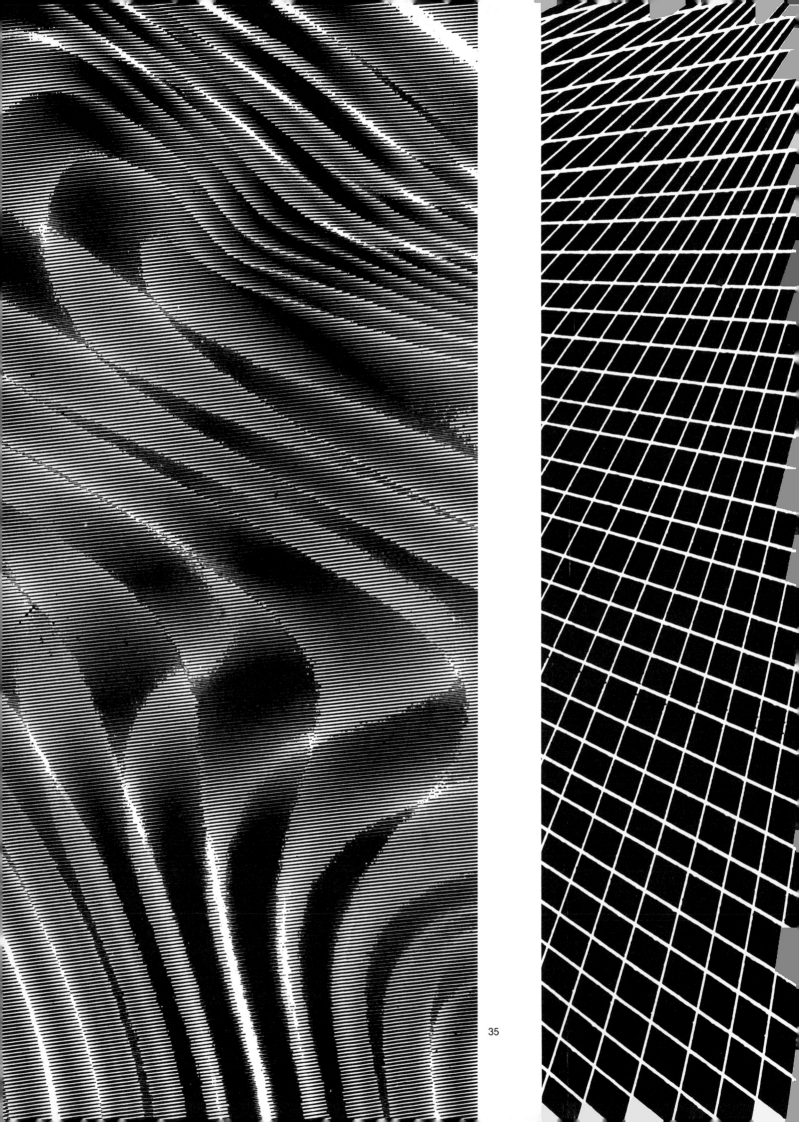

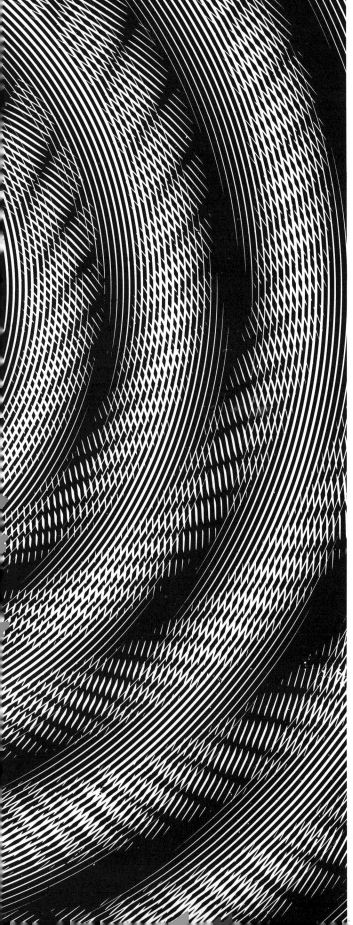

38

39

40

PAGE 53

42

44

45

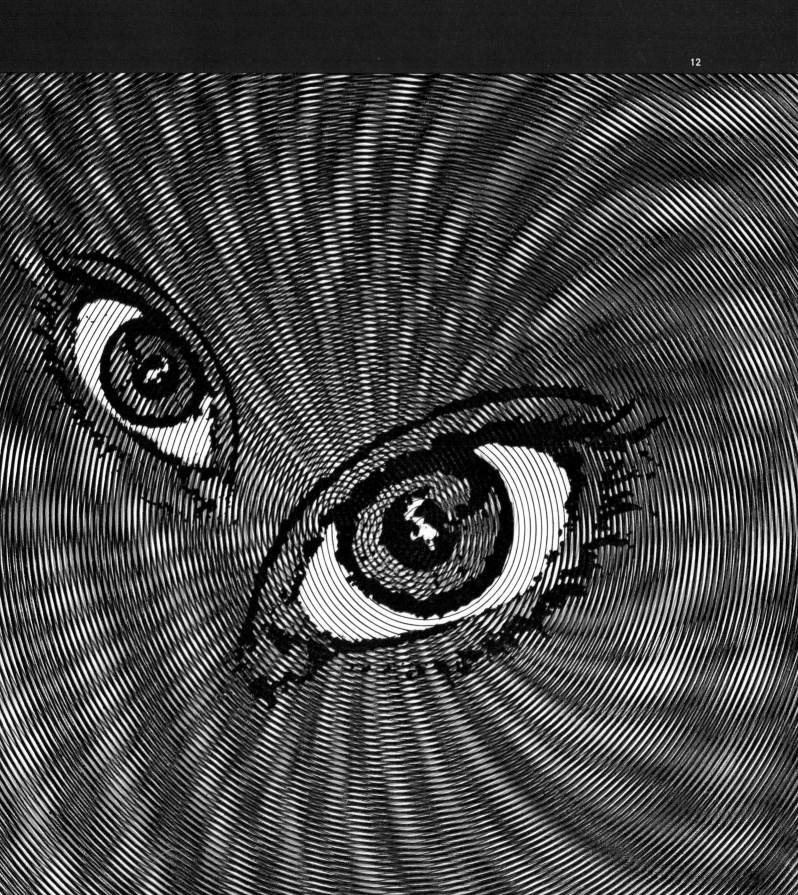

13

14

15

16

17

18 19 20

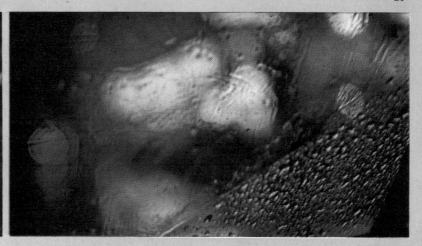

21

24

23

25

26   27

29

30

31

32

33

PAGE 65

52

53

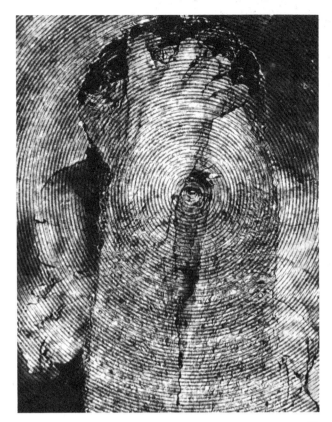

55

56

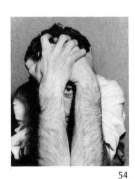

54

INTERPRETATION
4

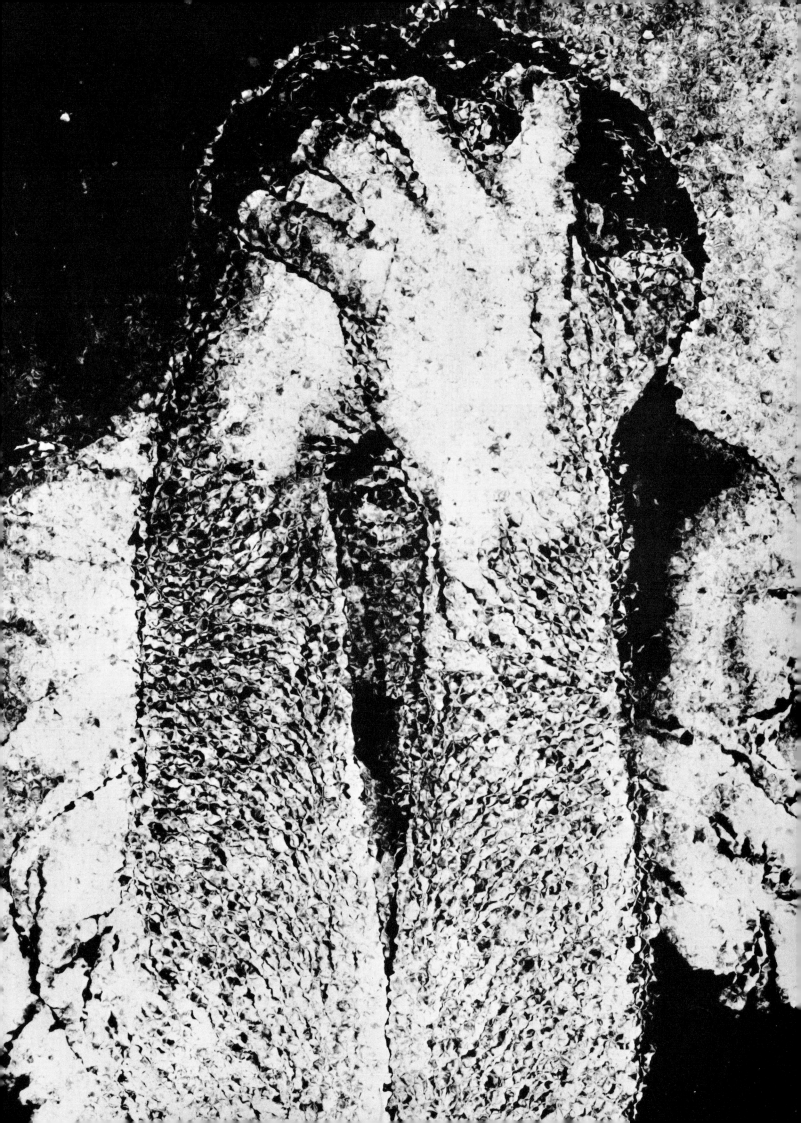

remember a story I was told many years ago about a farmer who receives a telegram from his son, who is away at a university. The farmer's glasses are broken, so he asks the mailman to read it to him. The mailman is annoyed by the request but opens the telegram. Then, using his most official voice, he roars through his mustache, "Daddy, send money immediately." The farmer is outraged. How dare his son speak to him with such disrespect. He determines not to send his son a penny.

A few days later, while the farmer is in the field tending his crops, the mailman drops another telegram at his house. Upon his return, the farmer notices the telegram and asks his twelve-year-old daughter to read it to him. The girl is aware of her brother's plight. "Daddy," she begins, her plaintive voice breaking into a sob, "send money," another sob, "immediately." The little girl is weeping mightily, and the farmer's eyes are filled with tears. Looking pleadingly at the little girl, he says, "Couldn't your brother have said it that way in the first place?" He sends the money off immediately.

Two interpretations of the same subject have taken place with entirely opposite reactions and results. An apparent and rather drastic change in the subject has taken place. Different characteristics have been emphasized by linking the subject to an emotional response. The harsh and indifferent voice of the mailman has been replaced by the sweet and emotionally charged voice of the little sister. The manner of reading the telegram acquired the value of the subject, while the real subject, the message, retired to the background. To translate this story into visual or photographic terms is not difficult, once we accept the fact that we possess the means of interpretation.

Let us consider only the range of interpretations that can be covered by printing the same image from very light to very dark, from very soft to very hard. Then let us consider the combinations, light-contrasty, dark-soft, and all the ranges in between. Very satisfactory and illuminating results can be achieved by printing on variable contrast paper and exposing through an arbitrary choice of filters. For a more intense effect, a series of film positives will have to be made and then sandwiched in register over a light box. They will have to be

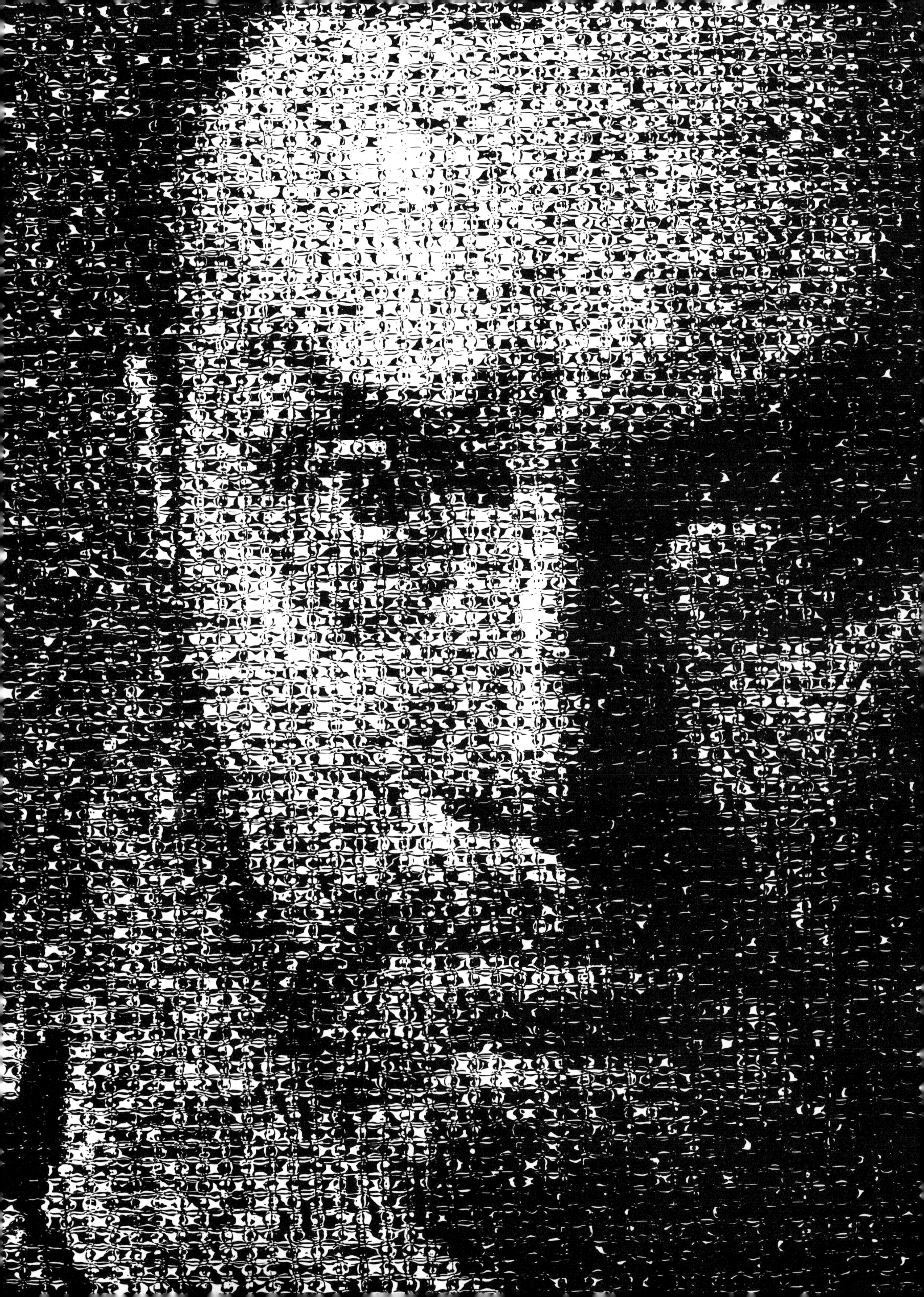

59

62

60

63

61

64

taped together, and a negative produced from them either by contact or enlarging. Prints are then made from this negative, which can be manipulated still further through the use of variable contrast papers. While going through a procedure of this sort, one cannot fail to discover characteristics inherent in the image that were not apparent in the straight photographic print or the original subject. In making these discoveries, photographic vision is amplified and can be applied at the time the original photograph is taken. The ability to preview pictures mentally has been enhanced, as has a keener awareness of the visual elements in any subject or scene.

Posterization is a process in which a negative is printed on litho film with increasing exposure in order to obtain a series of film positives covering larger and larger areas of black, until only the extreme highlights or catchlights remain white. From these, negatives are made; and two, three, or four are selected to be printed in register. The positive "separations" can be used by printing them on different colored diazo foils so as to obtain an additional visual solution to the original image. These same black and white positives can also be used for silk screen printing, too. There is an immense variety of applications of this process, which will be decided only by the amount of experimentation and ingenuity applied. To go back to the making of posterized positives, if a portrait has been chosen to be processed this way, you will experience a sense of discovery that will border on disbelief, the metaphysical, or a supernatural nightmare. This may sound exaggerated, I agree, and only by going through this experience will you come to agree with it. By posterizing the face of a young, beautiful woman—exposing litho film for two, four, six, eight, and ten seconds, say, until you achieve an almost black positive—you will end up with a series of very graphic positives. As the exposure increases, the young face begins to age steadily until it becomes incredibly old, tired, lifeless, and mummylike. Characteristics emerge that one never even suspected. The sweet expression begins to turn into bitterness, anger, and reproach. The sincere smile turns into a menacing grin. And the most frightening thing is that every picture is a "record" of what is really there, unseen until it has been brought out by the process. The whole thing looks somehow like a graphic presentation of a totally objective psychoanalyst. Or, better yet, a somaanalytic disclosure has been communicated. I do not believe that anyone can be confronted with such a series of images of himself and be stimulated to anything but a sensation of horror and despair. Nonetheless, the photographic practitioner will be able to select the proper stages of the process. By longer or shorter

78

exposure during overprinting, he will be able to emphasize or subdue characteristics in relation to his concept or to the concept he has been asked to illustrate.

The photographer will produce a number of interpretations and then choose the one he prefers. It is possible he won't like any, at which point he will have to start anew, taking advantage of all he has previously learned. It is most interesting, when you process a portrait of someone you know intimately, how well you recognize characteristics in the features that are hidden behind color and continuity of tone in the face in its natural habitat. It is remarkable how well we know how to emphasize, in our perceptions, the characteristics of a familiar face and how, in personal encounters, we subdue them into disappearance and grow blind to them. This amplification and elimination results from like, dislike, or some other less emotional prejudice. The same process in reverse is effectuated by Hollywood typecasting. We have become well acquainted with the Hollywood villain. When we meet a man or woman who conforms vaguely to the appearance of the movie scoundrel, we react with a certain amount of doubt, hesitation, or dislike. Our sense of observation has been weakened and our objectivity impaired. It is imperative to bear this tendency in mind during the process of interpretation so that you can arrive at the objective truth of posterization in any series you attempt.

The fine arts strive to bring out the inner or universal truth, which is beyond the obvious. From what has been said before about posterization, it would seem that an easy reference method has been devised. Not so. It is the sensitivity and desire to communicate an honest, worthwhile concept that will determine the value of the result and the justification for the use of any reference. When the assignment calls for a symbolic interpretation, that is, a visual formulation of a concept for which there is no ready image, the creative process has to take advantage of research in the elements involved. It must study the audience for which the picture is meant and utterly disregard all preconceived notions of what the photographic solution to the problem is expected to look like. Nevertheless, as necessary as this attitude of disregard is, it is certainly not alone the solution; it is only one of the means to the end. A perfectly conventional photograph might very well be the best solution, as long as the untried, unexpected, or unruly has been given a chance to compete and to lose out on the basis of unbiased judgment. Any product of serious art, commercial art, decorative art, art for art, art for pure fun, is the result

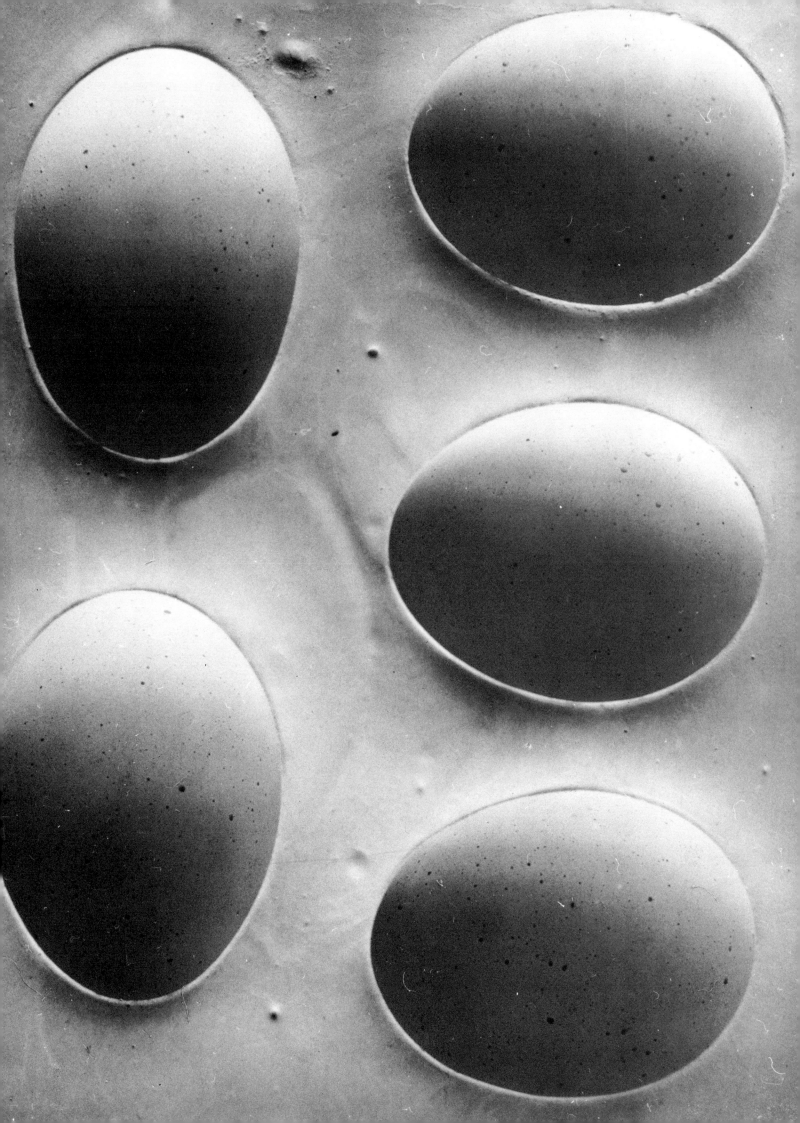

of interpretation. Good or bad, worthwhile or trite, haphazard or intentional, arrived at by guess or reflection, an interterpation it will be. The result will either speak for itself or will have to be helped by a caption—a lengthy, verbose, hypnotic rationalization. Because of this, the picture may become what it really is not, but just as convincing, which, sadly, is very often the case. A simple application of an unusual technique that will dominate the image may very often be the answer to a problem that looked very complex at first. A fork is an interpretation of a hand, a hammer that of a fist, and a deadly arrow benevolently shows us direction. These are simple or profoundly elaborate interpretations, depending on the amount of attention and thought one is willing to give them. To translate a continuous tone image into line is a technical interpretation, yet it may be powerful enough to stand up under the most sophisticated scrutiny. An interpretation can be a statement or merely a hint. In this context, it is the translation of a thought, concept, feeling, or emotion into form. It can simplify by eliminating detail, or it can elaborate by superimposing new elements. It can subdue or strengthen the emotional impact. The reaction of a viewer to an interpretation will depend on the nature of the interpretation. He will respond by reflecting the originator's concept, or will be stimulated to a range of emotions relating to his own experiences. As a rule, the more literal the interpretation, the less freedom it leaves for further interpretation by the viewer. This apparent limitation is often an asset rather than a shortcoming.

35

4 ◄

36

37

38

39

40

43

44

41   42

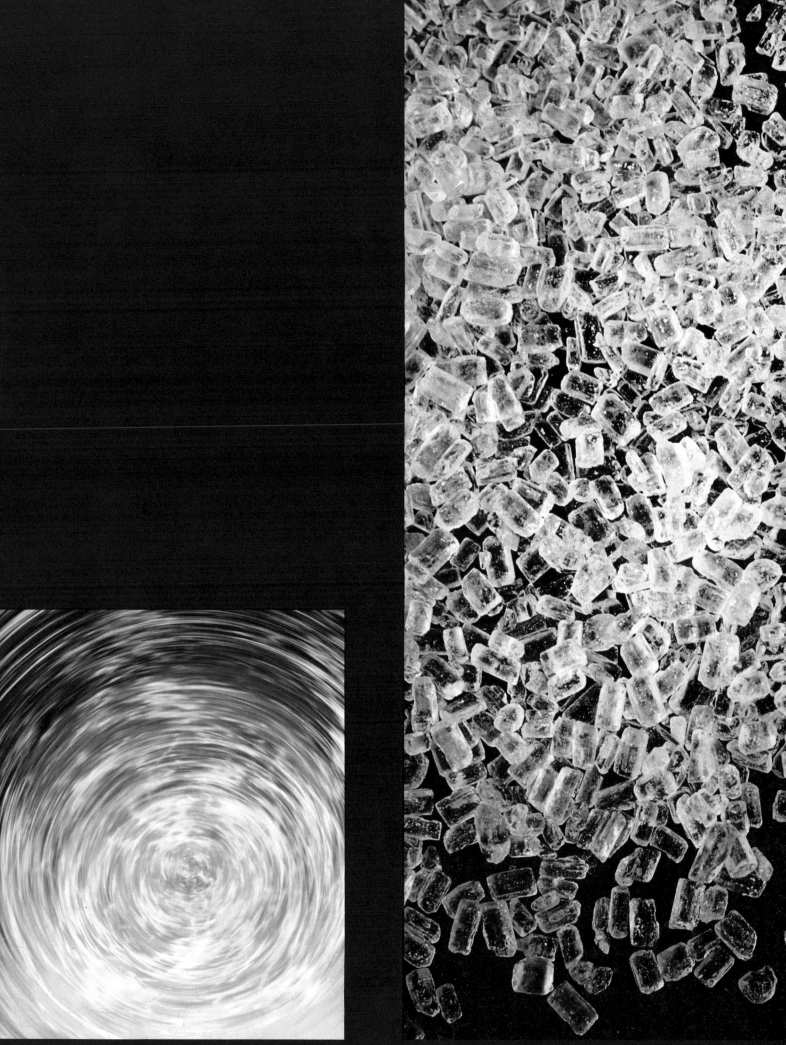

47 48

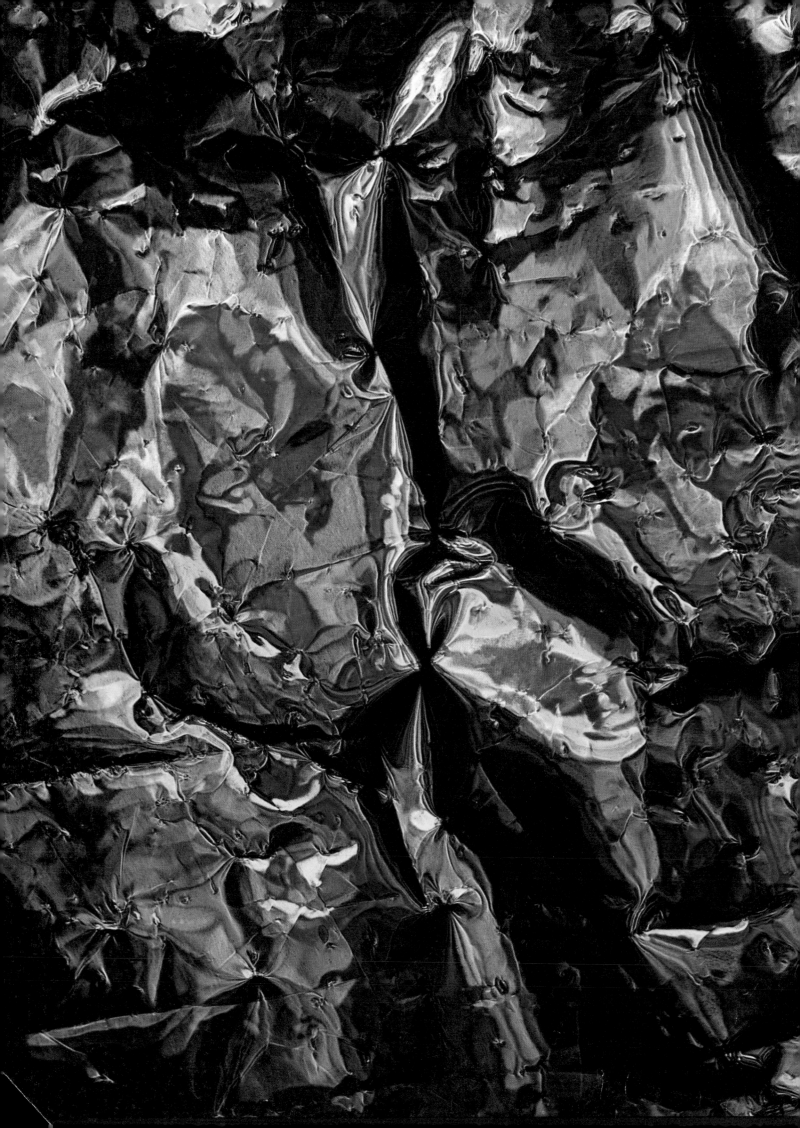

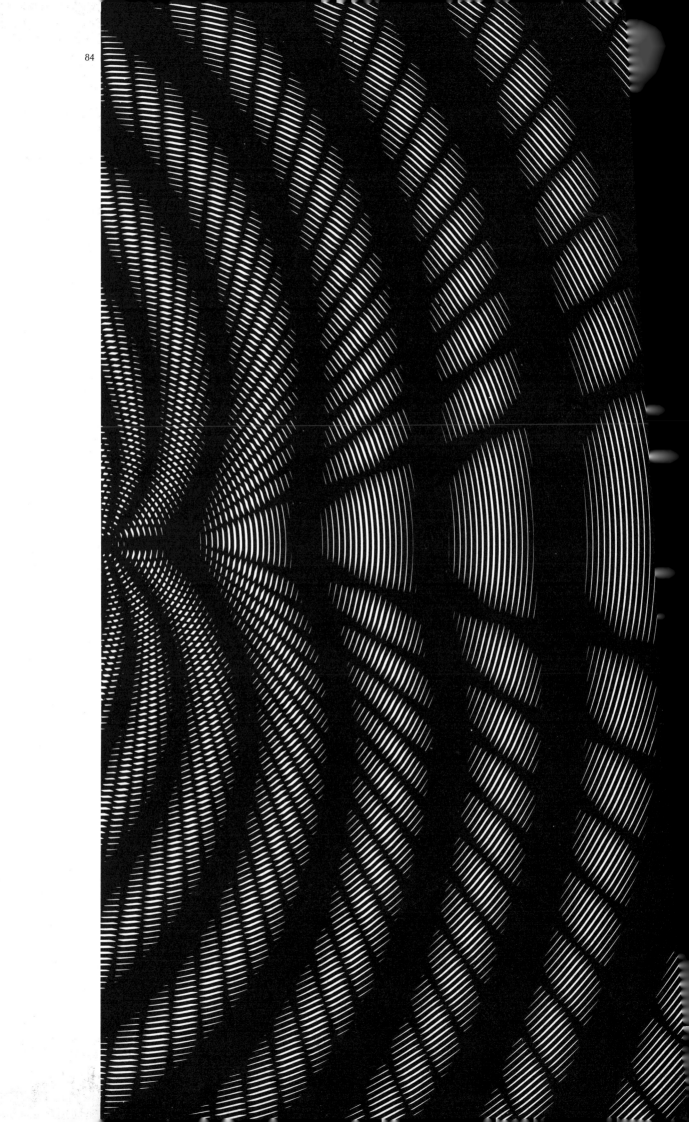

86

THE LASTING IMAGE

5

It is most intriguing to notice that in most photographic portraits of the Daguerreotype-Talbotype era, the subject displayed a forbidding grimness that seemd to imply a challenge to the world, a Weltschmerz and aggressive scorn. There must be a reason for this beyond the control of the photographer or the camera. Have you ever tried to smile or look pleasant for a full 60 seconds? Try it!

The more people there are in a portrait, the more static is the result, apparently because people are never in the kind of relationship that has been "captured." If any attempt is made to make the result appear candid, it is doomed to acquire the flavor of a Daguerreotype. I think it can be simply said that if the image tends to convey the intention of sound, or the sudden interruption of it, the result is bound to have a quality of obsolescence and an unplanned comic implication. In reviewing good portraits, we find that they live in and draw the viewer into an enclosure of silence.

A portrait is an image of an individual that presents him in the way he likes to be seen or accepted, the photographer sees him, or the photographer conceives the world in seeing him. If any of these conditions have been successfully captured, the result has to be a positive achievement.

There is a great deal of intimacy involved in the making of a portrait. This intimacy may be given by the sitter for many reasons. The subject may be acquainted with or impressed by the past accomplishments of the photographer. The photographer displays his awareness of the intrusion, yet is obviously on his way to producing a worthwhile result. The presence or absence of intricate photographic paraphernalia. The photographer's familiarity with some salient but not intrusive fact about the sitter. The photographer's charm, tranquility, or even aggressiveness.

As a rule, a personality in public life, in art, or science, is quite aware of his appearance. The only thing the photographer can contribute is his technical skill. Very often, the most important factor is a minimum of intrusion. To evaluate the degree of intrusion or management permissible is very difficult. Who can say how much without being judged too nosy or

PAGE 95

overbearing? Who can say how little without being judged too unsure of his own abilities?

We must, of course, be prepared to struggle with that savage animal called vanity, who attacks from people we least expect to possess it. Much integrity has fallen by the wayside, torn to shreds by its viciousness. Often it is wise to present flopped proofs, which, as a rule, are more acceptable; because that is how the sitter sees himself in the mirror and is used to the asymmetries of this view.

A portrait has to total the characteristic image of a person in relation to time, present or universal; to achievement, quality, intention, character, and value. The acting and directing of the subject are almost always confined to an imitation of "Old Masters" paintings, with all of their superb, overwhelming accent on static quality.

There must be no insolent factors involved in the making of a portrait. One can question, but not answer; one can amplify or whisper, but must not dictate or violate the trust. It is an exceedingly delicate matter.

PAGE 97

Distortion for the sake of distortion and investigation of how it can be applied for an occasional interpretation are, I think, good and valuable. However, these private experiments become an ill-advised cruelty when they are published in a magazine or book and are publicized as extraordinary achievements in the art of photography, or art in general. Thus, images that were intended only to explore means to an end become the ends in themselves. They are presented to the innocent as the well studied products of a very subtle mind and an ingenious talent simply because they were there, and a willing publisher with a good copywriter was ready. A photographic trend has been born.

Thus, when Aunt Milly objects to the fact that her proboscis is greatly exaggerated in a photograph, she is hushed down because of her ignorance of art. She retires sulking and offended. As a rule, I would say that distortion of living things (whether intended or not) results in ugliness. Let me amend that: continuous optical distortion of living things results in ugliness.

A gun is a pistol, a revolver, a rifle, a shotgun, a musket, a signal, a cannon, and among others, a toy. It can kill, wound, maim, cripple, defend, attack, protect, threaten, bully, deny, assert, rebel, be the arm of justice—or of crime, provide food or deny it. It can reach a point far away, or a large area close up. It can be the instrument of sorrow or of joy. It can signal distress or announce victory. It can attract help or disaster. It can destroy cities and provoke rebellions. It can take people's lives or pay homage to them. It can do so many more things, not the least of which is its ability, in toy form, to drive you crazy with its constant reminder of what it is not. I am not aware that a gun has ever been referred to as a creative tool. However, it occurs to me that there is a great affinity, in effect, to photography. The results of the comparison might not be immediate and drastic, but are certainly equal in intensity and importance. Regardless of the fact that the comparison holds fast in symbolic, technical terms, it is evident that the results are akin. Even the pot-pat of the toy gun reminds one of the editor who tries to sell us a photograph for what it is not, holster and trimmings included. The propagandistic assets of a photograph certainly compare favorably with the lethal effects of a gun. Advertising and public relations agencies are obviously well aware of that, whether the client is a manufacturer, a nation, a city, or even an international conspiracy.

Let us assume that we accept the comparison with the gun and proceed to consider just one of the corrosive misapplications of photography. Prostitution is prohibited in this country. I am not going to involve myself in discussing the merits of this, inasmuch as everybody knows that it exists anyway, without the benefit of sanitary supervision. It is advertised openly and constantly in magazines and books with inviting photographic displays of undressed women. The consumers of these widely-distributed magazines are led to believe that the contents of the publications represent a new, "in" society and are heralds of a "highly-sophisticated" and "cultured" mode of living. These promotional displays are often branded as art. Such publications are in existence for their glandular and erotic appeal, and are meant to stimulate desire for the subject. The implication, either in pose or expression, is, "Here I am, just come and get me." Not being able to comply with the invitation, the reader adapts it to his general attitude toward women, which is some kind of trembling contempt, but contempt nevertheless. The woman and girl is aware of these publications and the inherent implication that non-compliance is ridiculous. After all, it is publicly accepted. Mother, sister, brother are sent into oblivion, by comparison with the products displayed at the newsstand or bookstore.

In photography of the nude, a clear line can be drawn between the pornographic and the subtle. In one, the desire for the subject or the situation is stimulated. In the other, the reaction is of a general esthetic quality only remotely connected with erotic involvement. The photographer, or for that matter the publisher, should be aware of the lasting damage that these "come and get me" nudes, when given unlimited circulation, will effect on the relation between man and woman. Nothing prudish about this. No immediate explosion of moral turpitude or depravity will result from these displays, I imagine. But an attitude of disrespect cannot fail to be generated. The originators of these generalized advertisements for female promiscuity will sooner or later have to suffer the sneer of disrespect they have helped promote. Wife, daughter, son, or neighbor will suddenly display attitudes that will make him shudder and make him aware of his own responsibility. Photography can be destructive—and instrumental in producing lasting damage— much more than a painting; because, after all, a painting is the product of somebody's imagination. It may be true to fact or not. But a photograph is true. It is a record, an undeniable document of good or bad, of the beautiful or the lurid. It is an interruption of the continuum of time. It is a moment that has no past or future, but only a present. It is the lasting reference to emotions and to the relations between all things.

TEXTURE
6

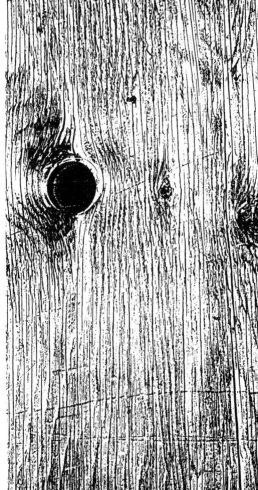

One of the main visual qualities, besides form, that makes us understand and accept things around us is texture. It implies the empirical association of touch, and in conjunction with it, temperature. If reduced to two dimensions, it becomes the pattern that defines and governs the surface of something. If we come close enough to it, it acquires the characteristics of a design, and even closer, those of an abstraction. A texture often has emotional implications. Peach, alligator hide, rock, sand, calm water, turbulent water, hedgehog, velvet, cotton, straw; all of these words, and their meanings in terms of texture, evoke undeniably different emotions. A texture invites exploration, even independently of the subject it is connected with. It is the question to the underlying structure. This seems to be atavistically so. The foot carefully explores the ground with an unfamiliar texture. This same reaction continues into intellect and emotion, regardless of how close or far these two are related.

Never before the advent of photography has texture been explored to the degree it has since, all the way to the anatomy of it, microscopically, macroscopically, or in any other way that would get close to it photographically. Nonetheless, it is amazing that with all that interest applied to the subject, little or only sporadic importance has been given to the pure visual enjoyment or the creative aggregates it carries with it. The emotional attachments of the human to texture date well before the advent of Dr. Freud, and are independent of attempted rationalizations. Texture is a visual subject in itself, as is an abstraction or a design. The correlation in a visual presentation is done either by the originator or selector of it, or by the beholder of the presentation.

A texture can be created photographically in the same way a design or an abstraction would, at which time it will become a mode of expression. The insertion of a texture into a representational subject without relating to the nature of the subject accomplishes a great deal, if applied and approached with finesse and artistic judgment. This might sound vague, but I doubt that it will be after one has had some unfortunate experiences or does some serious autodidactive research. If an application of texture reveals itself as evidence of technical

proficiency with the implication of trickery, it has failed. The first and absolute judge of this is the originator, who will either be accepted for his judgment or carry it with him, wherever time takes him.

A texture inserted into a representational subject will most probably invite a greater amount of emotional exploration of the subject than a straight photograph would. If the texture is permitted to dominate the image, however, the basic subject will become secondary, and instead of being carried more to the surface, will become submerged. In this context, I cannot help but be reminded of a cousin of mine, a big, strapping fellow, who greeted his beloved mother after a long absence and promptly crushed four of the poor woman's ribs with an overeager hug. A little overdone, his eager, uncontrolled gentleness was transformed in pain.

Photograph, by its original recording characteristics, carries with it also an invective quality, which has to be borne in mind whenever a deviation from those characteristics is attempted.

PAGE 102

105

101

ABSTRACTION
7

Destruction is a creative experience, probably because of the change of shape it produces. In modern art, this destructive tendency becomes quite obvious, especially if we assume that the academically representational is the expected, and the disfiguring product of the modern artist is the result. The motivations for this process appear to be relevant only to those who write or lecture about it, although these motivations seem to be quite obvious, especially since the advent of photography with its mechanically representational perfection and its apparently unjustified competition on a more conceptual level with handmade art.

The arts are in a constant state of upheaval at present. They fluctuate, grow, shrink, rebel, but they are dynamic and are in motion in a sort of "anything goes" way. This is good and must result in progress. The arts are crossing lines. One fuses with the other, if the originator feels like it. The classic and academic authority looks at itself in doubt. It is difficult not to be aware that quality and excellence will occasionally offend the establishment, particularly if originality of any kind, or even the kindling of it, is displayed. Unless someone in the establishment has decided to make the "discovery" and grant the seal of approval.

I am always amazed when an otherwise educated man is confronted with an abstraction and candidly states, "I'm sorry, but I just don't go for that stuff. I simply don't get it." What is there to get? This same fellow, flat on his back in a field, with his body on the bare ground, the grass touching his face, will gaze in ecstasy at the blue sky and the clouds and will, with abandon, open the gate to the universal tide of emotions, which his learned chastity would not permit him to do if he were faced with a framed abstraction. After a while, he will probably "sober up" and start to look for visual justifications: the cloud looks like a flying horse, or a flower, or the head of an old man. He will notice the tree branch between him and the sky, and the flock of birds in formation. If he were confronted with the fact that he had just been admiring an abstraction, he would say, "What do you mean? This is nature. This is the universe." Exactly. But, then, what isn't?

Acquiring a greater repertory of experiences and abilities

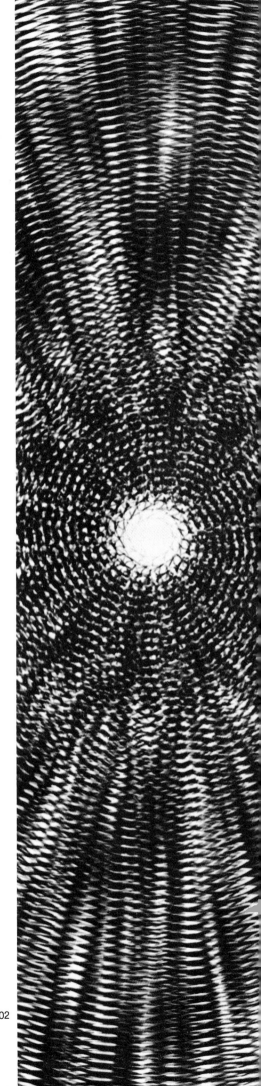

105

106

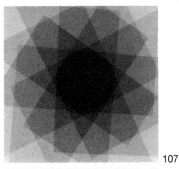

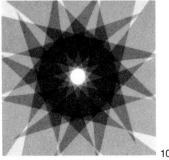

107

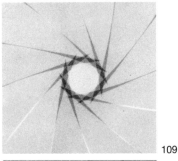

108

109

110

seems to be the privilege of a select few. That people react to a work of art by stating that they don't understand it and therefore don't like it is unacceptable. They fear that if they say they like or dislike a work of art, they will have to explain why. They fear that they will be required to prove their understanding of the work with a rational, learned justification. Can't they express an emotional response and communicate that, if necessary? Yet because of our system of art appreciation and education, we are made to fear our feelings and leave them open to question and doubt. We are made to believe that only what we are taught is valid.

A photographic abstraction of merit will be identified more readily that a reportage photograph, unless the latter has elements so outstanding, as to chronological happening or subject, that they are unmistakable. And this is rare. In order to define what is meant by abstraction, it would be necessary to determine what is not an abstraction, which I think is rather difficult. It could be simply something out of context.

An abstraction at times is an emphasis on a characteristic detail or on a whole. Thus the representative junction of two beams of a roof becomes an abstraction, and an abstraction of that would be the scheme of lines that are part of it. An expression of our past experiences, be it in color or black and white, is an abstraction. The visual representation of sentiment (emotion) is also an abstraction; consequently a summary or synopsis becomes an abstraction. As a matter of observation, words are abstractions; for instance, "cold" does not necessarily relate to a specific situation, but is important by itself in terms of emotional response to it.

A kaleidoscopic image, because of its symmetric qualities, governed geometrically by reflecting planes, will not qualify as an abstraction in the accepted meaning of the word. It is either an ornament or design. This indication is of some use when a photographic abstraction is attempted, for geometric schematizations seem to have no place in the origin of an abstraction. Random elements, meeting without any apparent rule and generating a new unit, will in all probability be more conducive to produce an abstraction. The originating of an extricated abstraction from a representational complex will be enhanced by viewing select elements in focus through the camera (ground glass), and varying the lens openings. Sometimes reality becomes secondary, or only a tool in the sequence of steps where an impression is intended to be communicated, or where the need to express is felt. As a rule, in an abstraction, the viewer should be made aware that there are no visual clues to be searched for, but that the emotions evoked in him are the solution; for an abstraction can convey a mood or emotion much more intensely than a representional photograph. That, however, does not hold true in a semi-abstraction, which will contain one or more recognizable elements and perhaps contribute as a visual comment.

111

112

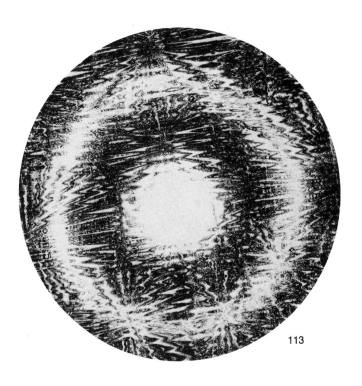

113

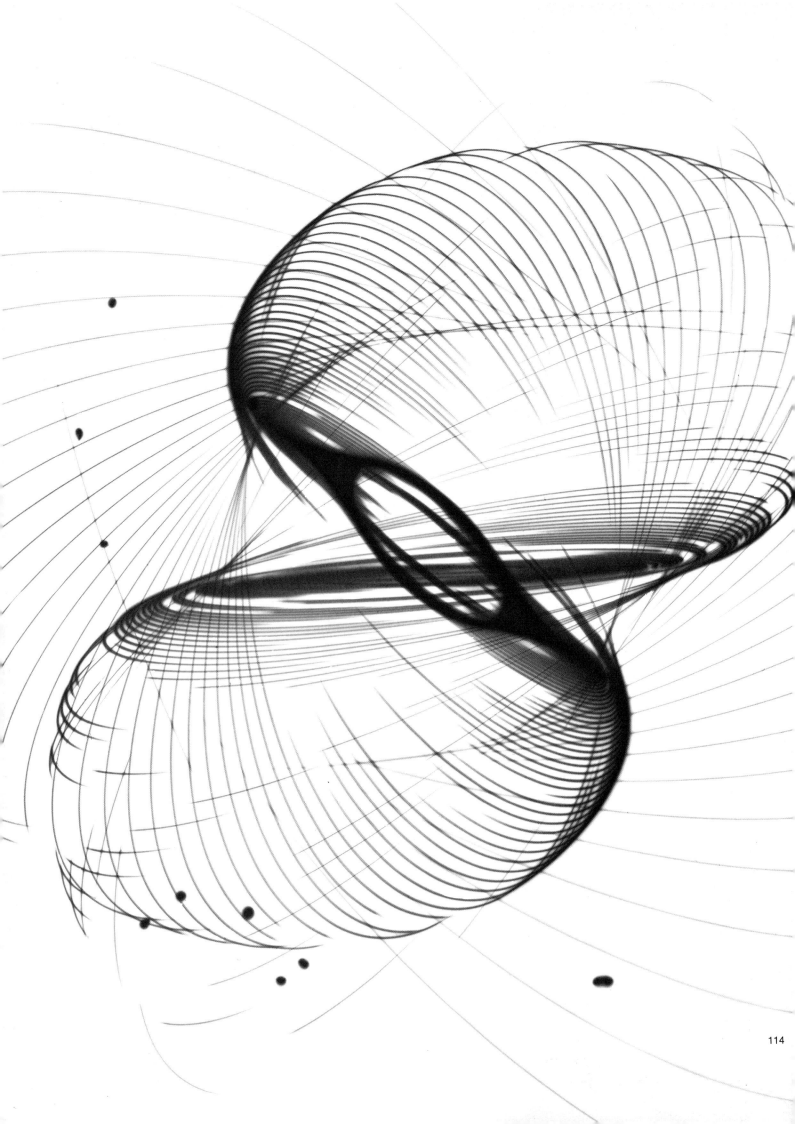

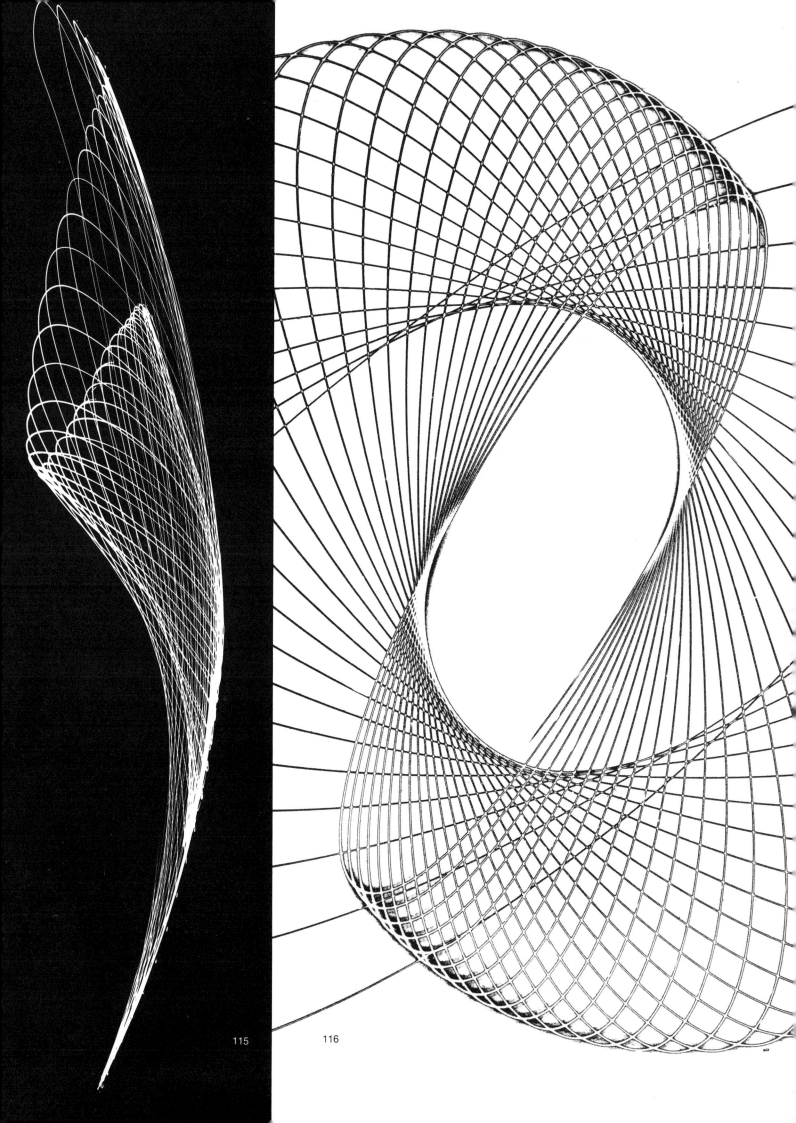

115

116

112

117

118

TIME
8

Every action requires time. The quantity allotted is determined by the nature of the action, or is predetermined by other means. Time has only one dimension, quantity; yet we have grown accustomed to refer to it in terms of quality, as relating to when, where, what, and who.

One qualitative evaluation is expressed in amounts of money, when compensation is considered. The result of such necessary financial reasoning in the trade has been some rather chaotic and disastrous conditions. Caste systems are established; pigeon-holing, with its inherent repression of ambition, becomes rampant. Consequently, pride in craftsmanship takes leave, and deterioration of quality takes over. This is the tendency, not the rule. Thus, let us say, a jar is to be photographed for an advertising agency. The art director calls the photographer and tells him he needs a picture of a jar. The instructions? "Well, you remember you did something like that for us a while ago!" And he lets the photographer know that he needs the picture in four hours, like the last time. A messenger takes the jar to the photographer; everything is set up and ready. He shoots it, develops, prints; three and a half hours later the pictures are at the agency. They are sent to the airbrushman or retoucher, who puts some zing into it. The whole thing is then inserted into the ad and sent to the printer. Net result? The photographer has once more proved that he is great for these rush-jobs," and has once more sealed his destiny. This is where he is going to stay; he will go no further. There probably wasn't any need for such a rush at all, but this kind of procedure has become routine. Besides, it does give a feeling of expediency and importance.

After such speedy mechanical experiences, an art director, editor, or anybody else who is assigning work to a photographer cannot but be influenced by them. For that matter, neither can the photographer. Then, when a more creative problem arises, to some degree it is dealt with, by contamination, in the same manner.

The resulting generous disregard for the time it takes to turn out a satisfying work of photography very often stems from the refusal of the assigner to get acquainted, even superficially, with the elements involved, let alone to consider the possibility that a reflective process exists. In photography the organization of time can be established only in terms of past experience: the constant elements versus the variables, the routine versus the experimental. Time and ingenuity have no mathematical relationship. Even when, because of past experience, ingenuity can be taken for granted, it is still subject to immediate circumstances. These could influence the mind into slowing down its release or expediting it. Constant practice and application of resourcefulness offer some assurance that it will be there when called upon, but it still remains a variable. As obvious as all this is, one does incline to disregard it. When a long ruminating process produces nothing but black despair, the photographer may be inclined to abandon the challenge, instead of just resting for a short while and then trying again. On the other hand, it seems advisable to plan the execution of a project on the reasonably short side, in reference to time, because of the stimulating tension this creates.

To be sure, certain things happen only at a certain time. More explicitly, one can make a trained dog jump, but one cannot make it have puppies, regardless of how well trained it is. In other words, if a photograph of these two situations has to be taken, the considerations of time are quite different. One can be taken right away and the other. . . well, who knows? Certain visual elements will be in an interesting relation only once and never again. If the picture is taken at that moment, it will have inherent in it the importance of this coincidence. The dimension of time can be felt in it. Photographic vision will induce the recognition of these timeless situations, which are still the result of the moment.

119

120

117

122

PRODUCTION
9

In order to reproduce a photographic original by any means of the graphic arts, certain consecutive steps have to be taken. The department in an organization concerned with the successful accomplishment of this transition is referred to as the production department, or "production" for short. Thus any problem pertaining to reproduction by any printing method is a production problem. The photographer who expects his work to be published should be acquainted with these problems, so that he can guide his work towards a more promising solution of them. Furthermore, he could develop methods that would facilitate production.

In most printing methods a continuous tone photograph will have to be first translated into a dotted image, from which the printing plate will be made. This dotted image is called "halftone" and consists of a regular grid of smaller and larger black dots on a white (or if film, transparent) background. These dots, when incorporated in the printing plate, will pick up ink selectively, according to their size, and will transfer it to the printing surface.

An image consisting only of pure black and pure white, without any intermediary grays, is called line copy. A pen and ink drawing is line copy. In the case of line copy, the reproduction is made without the interference of a halftone screen, and therefore will be less subject to changes that occur in the production and printing of a halftone. When a printed line copy is viewed with a magnifying glass it should look the same as the original. Often a contrasty continuous tone original will gain in impact and clarity if reproduced as line copy.

It is generally agreed that in each consecutive step in the reproduction of a photographic original, a loss of quality occurs. The amount of this loss will depend on the skill and craftsmanship of the persons involved in each step. On the other hand, in each of the steps, changes can be introduced with a view toward achieving a desired effect. The loss will then be only in terms of faithfulness to the original. Cost limitations, deadlines, union rules, etc., which are the concern of the production man, will often compel him to accept inferior reproduction. Such procedures result in the adoption of the minimum quality required by competition and a loss of pride in craftsmanship.

Some production problems can be minimized by photographic line-renderings of a continuous tone image. These renderings facilitate production and diminish the cost of reproduction. Line renderings are of great importance for newspaper reproduction, flexography (rubber plates), and for any printing on absorbent paper, which can take only very coarse halftones.

In order to produce a line conversion from a continuous tone original, one must first become familiar with litho films (Kodalith, Photolith, Reprolith, etc). The procedure involves repeated exposure through a texture screen onto a litho film. Part of the exposure can be done without the interference of the screen in order to assure solid blacks. The screen should be of a random pattern if it consists of dots or cross-hatch, as any regular pattern will result in an undesirable moiré effect. Some of these screens are available in art supply stores; others are the products of individual ingenuity. Parallel line screens are handled differently, as it is advisable to introduce a distance between the screen and the litho film. The thickness of a pane of glass could be a good starting point. Varying the aperture of the enlarger lens will influence the apparent contrast of the resultant image. Some variations can be affected by varying the exposure-development ratio. The resulting positive is contact printed onto a line negative on litho film, which in turn is used to make an enlargment or print on a #5 or #6 paper.

In making a line conversion, it is advisable to keep in mind that one is tampering with the characteristics of the original. A line conversion could very well be (and often is) an interpretation in meaning too, because it brings to the surface some less obvious elements in the original. Some characteristics will be emphasized, others under-played or completely deleted, which is just as well, as long as one has learned how to master this interplay and can relate it to the desired result. Posterization, as mentioned in the chapter on Materials, is another method of line rendering particularly applicable to silk screen printing, posters, etc. Some extremely interesting results can be achieved by combining a textured conversion with one or two stages of the posterization process.

Tone-line is a process in which a (flat) positive is made in contact with the original negative. These are then taped together, back to back, in register. After this, the sandwich is put in a printing frame with litho film. This is then put on a turntable, and while rotating, is exposed to a light (5 watts) about three feet away and at an angle of 45 degrees. The result should be a line positive that will incorporate the outlines and texture characteristics of the original. A negative of this is made and copied or enlarged or combined with any other line rendering, or even a continuous tone.

If the production man has problems with the reproduction of black and white, he has four times as many when it comes to color. Four separations are involved, to be printed in register. A set of progressive proofs serves as a guide in correcting the separations. The photographer should make it his business to get acquainted with several sets of progessive proofs. A great deal can be learned by studying them and realizing the values of the four components that make a color reproduction. If he can be present when such a set is checked by a production man, so much the better. Having acquired some knowledge about separations, and the intricacies of the procedure, the photographer will eventually be able to apply himself actively.

126

The knowledge of separations will become indispensable should the photographer decide to get involved in "line color separation" work, after having assimilated the black and white conversion technique. Line color separations are becoming increasingly important in newspaper color printing—ROP as it is called in the trade—for the technical advantages this process offers, plus the gain in visual impact a line rendered color print acquires. Once line color separation has been mastered, the next step would be to get involved in color transversion. Color transversion is a process very much akin to line color separation, except that the original is not a color transparency but a black and white negative or print. In other words, a black and white photograph is turned into a line separated color image. From the black and white negative, a set of varied line conversions is made—different in the amount of black they will incorporate. Then different colors are assigned to the line conversions, considering them as line separations, either arbitrarily or in reference to a fictitious progressive proof. These positives are printed on some color proofing material (Diazochrome, Oza-chrome, 3M Color Key, etc.) according to the colors assigned. These color foils are then taped together in register, and the result can be viewed. It is amazing how close one can get to an approximation of the colors that would have been there had the original been in color instead of black and white. Even when the resulting color image has become so stylized that its colors do not relate at all to the natural colors, the experiment will have been worthwhile, if for no other reason than for its value as a variation and a visual adventure. As photography progresses, art directors, editors, designers, and production men will learn to rely on photographic vision as a generative agent of an immense number of techniques, to be conjured up simply by defining their scope.

SELECTIVE VISION

10

The owner of the repair shop to which I brought my car for some adjustments pointed to my portfolio case.

"You an artist?" he asked casually.

"I like to think so," I answered in the same manner.

"What do you do?"

"Photography."

He lit up all over. He stammered a moment, searching for words. "Oh, come on, you must be kidding." He was so excited he had to swallow hard before continuing. "I'm a camera bug too, you know."

He proceeded to describe to me his arsenal of cameras—a veritable battery of lenses, enlargers, exposure meters, strobes, and all sorts of other gadgets that would fill the pipe dreams of any photographer and would be sufficient to equip a whole battalion of sophisticated professionals. He washed his hands and brought out a file box of slides.

"Come on," he said. "Have a look and let me know what you think about them."

I glanced through his mass of perfectly exposed 35mm color transparencies. Immaculate exposure; but otherwise, nothing.

"Nice," I said.

"No, don't," he replied. "I know. Garbage, that's what it is. But that's the best I can do. I guess I just don't have it in me."

Somehow, I grew impatient, almost angry. He sensed it. "Please, show me some of your stuff."

I put my portfolio case on his bench. Gingerly, he began looking through my work. His eyebrows lifted slowly until it seemed they would get lost in his hairline. "These are photographs?" he asked. "But how?"

"I'll tell you," I enunciated gravely. "Fancy, thought, research; sweat, thought, sweat. And all of it sprinkled with the joy of doing it."

"How I wish I could do things like that," he said again and again as he went through my work. "Why can't you?" I asked. "Is there any subject in my transparencies that is less familiar to you than to me?"

"No, but I still say I can't take pictures like those. I just don't see the way you do."

"Not so," I insisted. "You recognize and appreciate them

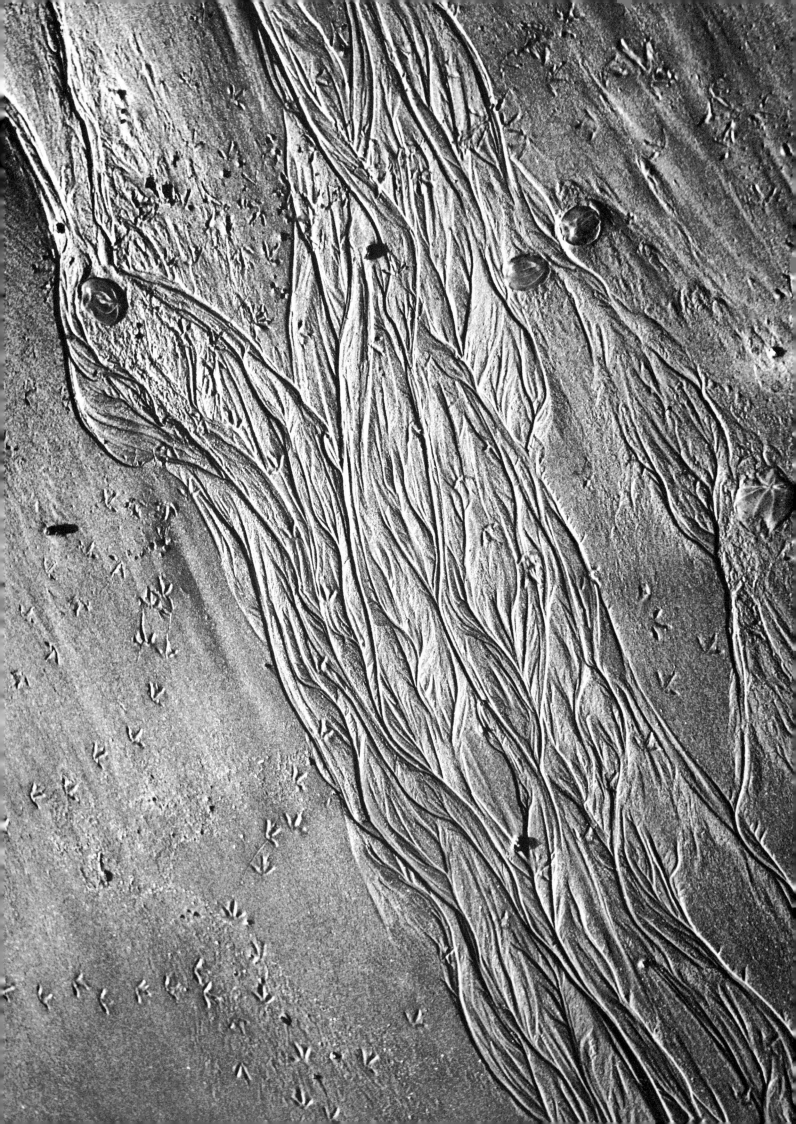

when you look at these slides. Why can't you do the same when you study the ground glass on your SLR?"

"I guess I just never trusted myself to do it, so I never even tried." His face brightened slowly. "Boy," he said with a grin, "if I ever took pictures like these and showed them around they'd probably say I'm cheating."

"Fine," I said. "You're visualizing pictures now. Do it on the ground glass of your camera, or even without it, but do see things for their own sake; for their colors, their form, their design. Move in close, and closer still. Change your camera angle. But see selectively; respond to your subject; visualize how the picture would turn out if you changed aperture. Forget about what you are supposed to do. Just get involved, be stimulated by your own feelings. Enjoy yourself!"

Then his assistant interrupted to tell me that my car was ready. I left, with a promise to return in a few weeks, to see what sort of pictures he took in response to my short-order lecture. When I did return in about a month, I was delighted, and frankly, in spite of my hopes and convictions, amazed. The pictures he had come up with were simply unbelievable in their startling contrast to the ones he had first shown me. Now there was meaning, imagination, vision.

No, I am not attributing the results to any messianic influence on my part. A simple change of attitude took place; the man began to think in positive terms. He changed from "How can I?" to "How can I not!" With his inhibitions removed, his creative potential was able to emerge without shame, and he was able to apply all his technical knowledge in an excitingly new way. This episode, typical of many others I have gone through, was largely responsible for my desire to put my convictions into a book and to bring my message of the creative potential in everybody to an audience far larger than I could find in chance encounters.

Selective vision is the ability to extricate a visual unit out of a complex that would keep that unit from emerging. It is more than cropping in enlarging, though that is part of it. In practical application, selective vision will take advantage of selective focusing, change of viewpoint, choice of exposure, panning, and any other means adaptable to the separation of the different elements. The quantity and quality of past photographic and esthetic experiences will be instrumental in its development. In other words, it is not an ability that will descend upon the photographer as a result of a wish. It is true, however, that being aware of its existence will promote its realization; awareness spurs the search. Once this ability has been acquired, it will manifest itself in subjective expression. It will not easily be lost.

130

PAGE 128

132

PAGE 129

133

136

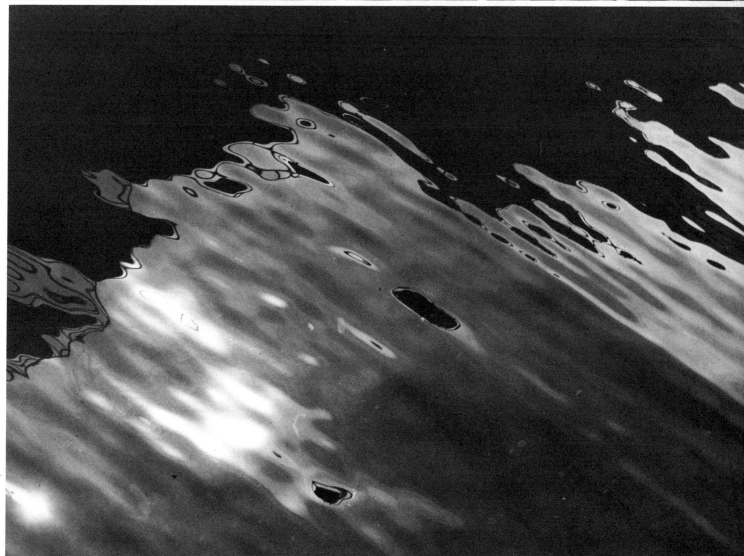

137

PAGE 132

138

139

140

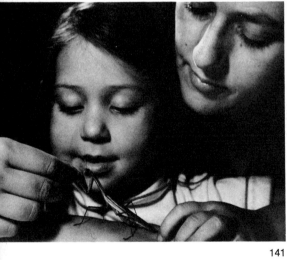

141

142

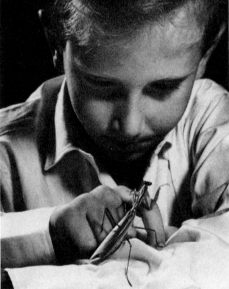

143

THE ASSIGNMENT
11

An assignment is a procedure in which a photographer accepts or imposes upon himself the obligation to produce work or follow a process based on a "concept" established. The difference between a self-imposed assignment and one coming from the outside should be evident only in terms of time, not in terms of quality or intensity of involvement. This is mentioned not in order to pontificate, but to point out the danger of turning a creative process into a routine procedure. Stagnating the dynamics of the creative process for expediency, or any other reason that might be convenient or seem appropriate at the time, could very well lead into the rut of mediocrity. A few "Oh, that's good enough" experiences might, through contagion by sequence, develop into a habit, putting an end to individual freedom and turning an artist into a psuedo-artisan.

This, of course, could also happen during a self-appointed assignment, induced by the tedium of an experiment that presented a few unpleasant setbacks in its course. The fact that there are "two" parties involved in an assignment from the outside is of major importance, though very often ignored and neglected. The assigner will engage a photographer on the basis of his past work, his portfolio, his reputation, or any other indication that he is the right choice. This delicate decision, being subject to error, is of far-reaching influence to the whole field of photography. The tendency of playing safe and resorting to specialists, or just simply reliable but routine performers, results in the perpetuating of mannerisms and trends that inhibit any liberal, inspired progress.

On the other hand, a portfolio will only too often be judged by what is in it in the way of subject matter, and not by the imagination and creative potential it displays. In spite of the fact that the art director, editor, or whoever is deciding is greatly inclined to use a photographer, he will decide against him because the particular subject of the assignment does not appear in the portfolio. Then again, he might become over-enthusiastic and start believing that he has found the magician who will solve all his problems with a click. This will result because of the absence of empathy so necessary in a creative symbiosis.

The photographer will occasionally find himself in complete

51

52

58

53

54

55

56

57

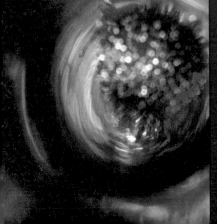

62

63

65

64

66

67

69

70   71   74

72   73

68

75

76

77

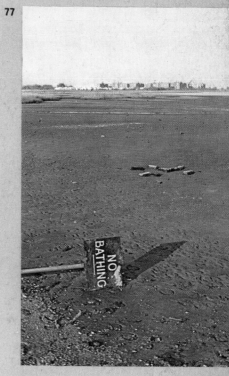

NO
BATHING

78

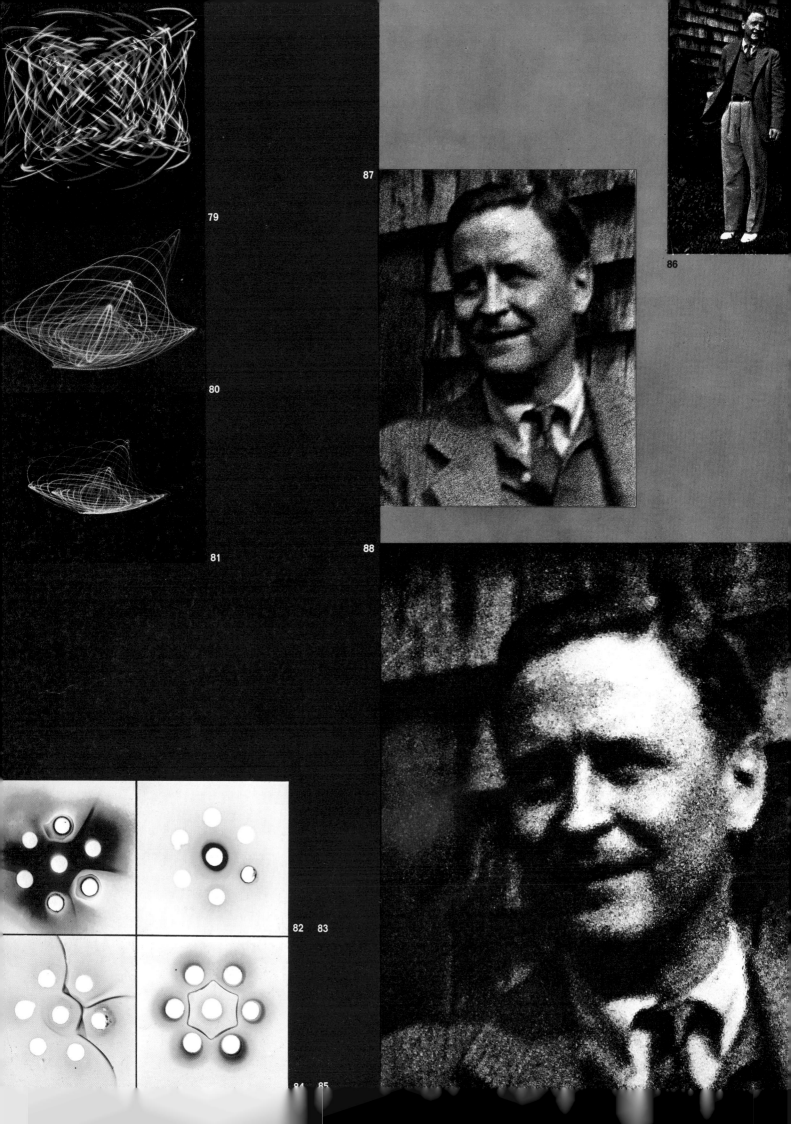

79

80

81

82   83

84   85

86

87

88

147

jeopardy on an assignment because of prohibitive time limitations and technical, physical, and circumstantial difficulties that cannot be conquered by any amount of ingenuity. This will occur, mostly, because of the photographer's assumption that the assigner is familiar with the basic technicalities of photographic procedure and that he is also acquainted with the circumstantial elements involved in the assignment. The assigner might not even care about familiarizing himself with these things, because he is, after all, dealing with a magician who knows no obstacle. Though this does not usually occur, it occurs often enough to suggest that a great deal of the success of an assignment hinges on the assigner as much as on the photographer. It can be assumed that if the photographer has been chosen for his ingenuity and creative genius, he will have enough integrity and ethical fortitude not to take advantage of his expertise for monetary reasons by suggesting the existence of some imaginary difficulty.

When a photographer is called on an assignment, in order to illustrate or develop a visual or an editorial concept, the job basis is agreed upon with a deadline or a day by day (fee) basis. A deadline is a time limit established, within reason, in relation to the requirements of the assignment and in approximation of similar past experiences. On a day by day editorial assignment, involving unexpected elements and circumstances that are subject to influences beyond the control of the photographer or the assigner, the time element becomes quite unpredictable. It should be considered a variable with consideration for the unforeseen and based on mutual trust.

I was once assigned to illustrate an essay on air pollution. The idea was to photograph, in a neighboring town, the belching factory smokestacks that polluted the air of our city. I remembered vividly having almost choked to death while driving on an elevated highway through that town not too long before I got the assignment. The memory persisted—the green, yellow, and ominous, light, red-brown color of the gases exuding from the smokestacks and sweeping over the crowded slow-moving traffic on the highway. Quite a frightening experience! Illuminated by the lights of the highway and the headlights of the cars, the smokestacks and the factory buildings looked like scenery out of a vicious surrealistic movie. I remembered also how frantically I looked for an exit from the highway, and that there was none for a long while, until the danger zone was far behind. With these memories, and the hope that I would some day be in a position to comment on this outrage, I accepted the assignment.

I was given a fairly precise itinerary. When I started out early in the morning I was met by one of the most brilliant days I ever experienced in these parts. The air was crystal clear and the visibility was limited only by the horizon. Fate smiled at me, I thought. What a background against which to catch a few spewing, billowing smokestacks in the act. On the way to my destination I found myself conceiving ways to dramatize visually the irresponsibility of the offenders. Near my destination, the highway reaches a high point far above anything around for many miles. I stopped at an emergency landing. Before me

extended the valley with its hundreds, maybe thousands, of factories. The air was clear and I could see all of them below me. I had only to pick; the choice was mine; the hunt was on. Yes, the air was clear, crystalline, splendid; inviting one deep breath after another.

Suddenly, I became aware. My desperate eyes started searching, perusing, analyzing. I grabbed for my binoculars, only to increase my exasperation. Not one thin thread of smoke; not even so much as a quiver of hot air; nothing but clear, crystalline, breath-inviting purity. The rest of the day I looked for at least one measly smoke-puffing smokestack. Not even one. The next three days were just as beautiful and just as smokeless. My inquiries were met with suspicious looks and cryptic answers. Everybody seemed to be hiding something from me. A paranoid experience to say the least.

Finally I managed to take a series of pictures just as the sun had set of a family of four sister smokestacks that were quite busy (but not busy enough). I was promptly seized by two guards and ushered into the administrative building of the factory, where I was to answer for my crime. It took me all of fifteen minutes to prove my innocence by showing my publisher's letter, requiring assistance in the assignment. The plant manager apologized. I growled and left, still with the feeling that I would be shot in the back. Everybody was quite confused and embarrassed, including me.

As I was returning to the car, night was slowly descending. I noticed a heavy black layer of smoke on the crimson horizon. It was only then that I remembered that my nightmarish experience on the highway had taken place at night. Next morning a guard at the entrance gate to an oil refinery listened to my plight with amusement. He informed me, laughingly, that of course I couldn't see any smoke, as the factories start to operate their smokestacks the moment the sun sets, in order to avoid penalties and fines; the idea behind it apparently being that the authorities are not so touchy after dark sets in. How that helps to get rid of air pollution beats me, but that's how it is.

It took almost five days on this assignment to find out that a specific technical method had to be found to combat an unforeseen circumstance that one could not become aware of beforehand. It goes without saying that such empirical traumas are frustrating to the point of despair. Nevertheless, it seems that they are unavoidable at times and necessary in a profession in which one apparently has to be aware of everything and has to get close, and acquainted with, things that a bystander doesn't even know exist.

150

151

152

INTEGRITY
12

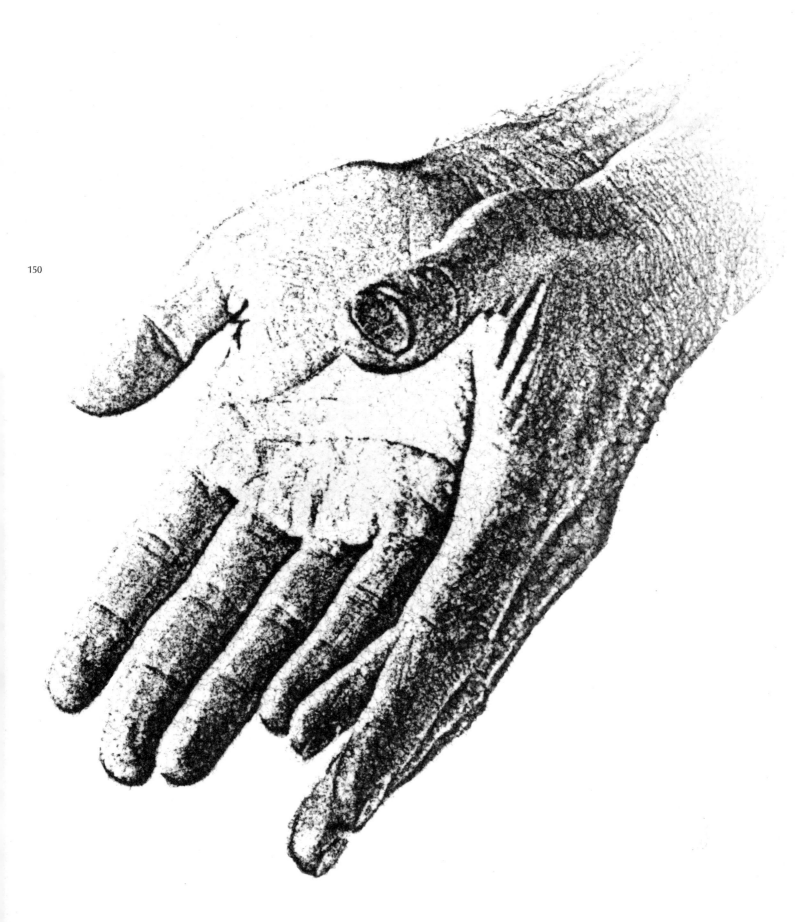

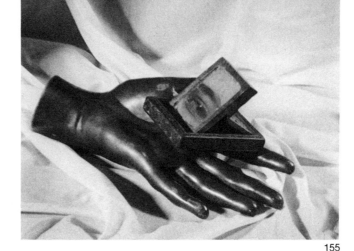

Integrity. What a beautiful word. Especially when spoken in the presence of children. If we intend to exercise integrity, or what is left of it after we have made our compromises, then let us keep on using the word for want of a better. Integrity is the opposite of conformity. It is the subconscious of human qualities and virtues brought to the surface. When it exists, it does not have to advertise itself, for it becomes evident without having to declare its presence. It will manifest itself in spite of circumstances, in spite of the individual himself. Everybody is born with it, and many devices are applied from the outside to submerge it. One can reacquire it by wanting it. The integrity of the artist will eventually express itself in a personal style.

A silly habit of brainless, inflexible following of a trend or dogma is not a substitute or proof of integrity. If it were, a trained flea could lay claim to it. Nor is insistence on a learned or acquired prejudice a demonstration of integrity; it is, on the contrary, an induced disability of the mind to function universally in reference to its full potential. More often than not, such prejudice is used to eliminate something one is afraid of or cannot cope with. When a prejudice is challenged by progress, or even the simple process of evolution, it will respond by parading under the banner of integrity. Thus, the challenger becomes a blasphemous villain. The extreme photographic purist, in defense of his laziness to investigate and explore, will

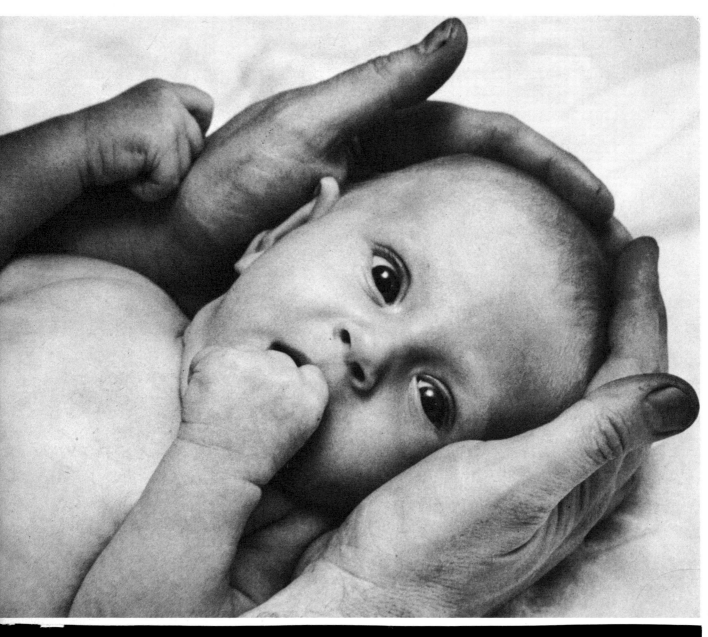

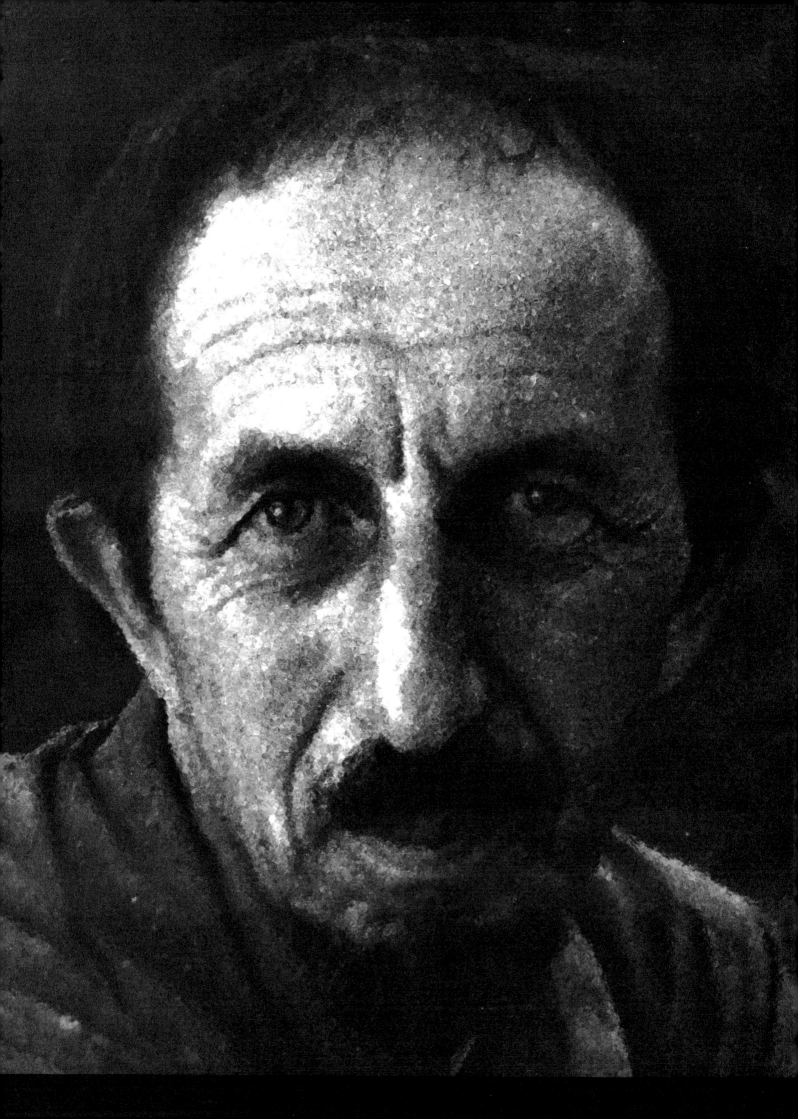

rotten one, a parasitic leech on the back of the universe. Any virtue, to him, is for suckers. On the other hand, the coward who suffers hell for his cowardice is really a hero in disguise, and his moment of glory will come. He lives for the moment when he will assert himself. He is pregnant with integrity. He meets the carefully taught axioms of convention with squinting eyes, judging them for what they are. He cultivates and develops the freedom of choice. Once he has achieved it (as much as this is ever possible) he can activate his own personality. In terms of photographic vision, he will see as he wants to see (not as he is trained to). He will photograph, extricate, abstract, manipulate, condense, dilute, add, subtract or do whatever he feels he must, to arrive at the image he has visualized. Whether this is done for the joy of sheer visual delight, or to comply with an urge to express, is of no consequence. He is a coward no more.

It would seem that integrity, in the context discussed, would be in direct conflict with professional photography or assignment from the outside. Not at all. If the concept of integrity is honestly evaluated, it will become apparent that it is flexible in quality, direction, and in quantity. Thus, one can have this kind or that kind of integrity, one can have a little or much. Just to dispel the frown on the dissenting brow, consider the accepted, dignified statement: "He is a man of great integrity." Doesn't that imply that there are others, almost as respectable, but of lesser integrity? Again: "His integrity as a pioneer in ———— is beyond any doubt." Quality, direction! It follows that we have accepted variables. When an assignment from the outside comes along and we accept it, the responsibility to comply with the requirements within the framework of our own makeup becomes part of integrity. Any compromise or adapting of oneself has been done in accepting the assignment. After that, the ethics of responsibility have to work hand in hand with what is left of the original integrity. A new integrity has been appropriated. The deceit is only in not accepting this as an adult, honest way of things, as they really are. Integrity is a rationally produced, lasting attitude, not to be mistaken for sincerity. Sincerity is a personal thing of the moment: it is the sum of directness that one can afford in relation to his emotional makeup at the time.

PAGE 155

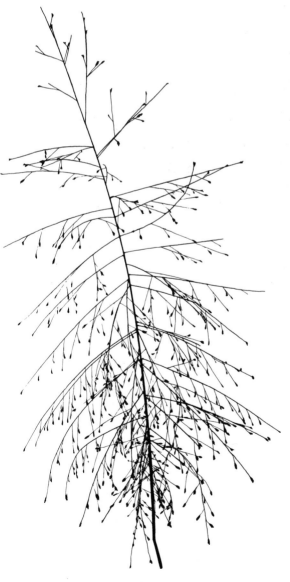

INDEX TO PHOTOGRAPHS

The index below gives some information on the techniques used in making the photos in this book. The bold face numbers correspond to the numbers next to each photograph. The roman type indicates the photographer's technique, the italic type the printing reproduction process.

COLOR

1 Combination of black and white line rendering with photographic abstraction in color. *3-color process halftone and black and white line*

2 Abstraction. Colored light sources and reflections. Optical variants introduced by set of lenses of different focal lengths. *4-color process*

3 Abstraction. Colored light sources with opaque interference. *4-color process*

4 Abstraction. Colored light sources and reflections. *4-color process*

5 Abstraction. Part of plastic dish photographed with colored lights. *4-color process*

6 Abstraction. Part of plastic dish photographed with polarized white light. Polarizer on lens and light. *4-color process*

7 Abstraction. Colored light sources and reflections. *4-color process*

8 Abstraction. Colored light sources and reflections with opaque interference. *4-color process*

9 Abstraction. Colored lights and reflection. *4-color process*

10 Abstraction. Colored lights. *4-color process*

11 Symbolic semi-abstraction. Infrared gas heat. Ceramic tile element, reflected colored light and reflections. *4-color process*

12 Symbolic abstract design to illustrate the concept of dreams, as it appeared in Newsweek magazine. *4-color line*

13 Autumn. Water reflections. 2¼ x 2¾. Ektachrome. *4-color process*

14 Sunset reflections. 35mm single-lens reflex. Kodachrome. *4-color process*

15 35mm single-lens reflex. Ektachrome. *4-color process*

16 35mm single-lens reflex. Kodachrome. *4-color process*

17 2¼ x 2¼ twin-lens reflex. Ektachrome. *4-color process*

18 35mm single-lens reflex. Kodachrome. *4-color process*

19 35mm single-lens reflex. Kodachrome. *4-color process*

20 Street lights in rain through automobile windshield. 35mm single-lens reflex. Ektachrome. *4-color process*

21 Street at dusk in rain photographed through automobile windshield. 35mm single-lens reflex. Kodachrome. *4-color process*

22 35mm single-lens reflex. Kodachrome. *4-color process*

23 35mm single-lens reflex. Kodachrome. *4-color process*

24 35mm single-lens reflex. Kodachrome outdated 2 years. *4-color process*

25 35mm single-lens reflex. Ektachrome. *4-color process*

26 35mm single-lens reflex. Kodachrome. *4-color process*

27 Child with red bowl. 2¼ x 2¼ twin-lens reflex. Ektachrome. *4-color process*

28 Water reflections. 35mm single-lens reflex. Kodachrome. *4-color process*

29 3-color variation of #31, blue, yellow and black printers. *2-color process plus black printer in line*

30 3-color variation of #31, yellow, red, and black printers. *2-color process plus black printer in line*

31 4-color transversion of black and white #52. The three line color separations were here printed as halftone, while the black printer was used as originally rendered in line. Kodalith. Ozachrome. *3-color process plus black printer in line*

32 3-color transversion of black and white #53. Arbitrary line separations (blue, red, black) were used for this print. Kodalith. Ozachrome. *3-color line*

33 Continuous tone variation of #32. Soft stipple rendering introduced in process.

34 Abstraction. Colored lights and reflections. *4-color process*

35 35mm single-lens reflex. Kodachrome. *4-color process*

36 Water reflection through fence. 35mm single-lens reflex. Kodachrome. *4-color process*

37 35mm single-lens reflex. Kodachrome. *4-color process*

38 2¼ x 2¼ twin-lens reflex. Ektachrome. *4-color process*

39 Sailboat rigging. 35mm single-lens reflex. Kodachrome. *4-color process*

40 35mm single-lens reflex. Kodachrome. *4-color process*

41 Miniature optical prisms on wire mesh photographed under colored lights. 4 x 5 Ektachrome B. *4-color process*

42 Abstraction. Pigments in motion. 4 x 5 Ektachrome. *4-color process*

43 Abstraction. Textured glass. 4 x 5 Ektachrome. *4-color process*

44 35mm single lens reflex. Kodachrome. *4-color process*

45 Colored light sources and optical interference of reflections. 4 x 5 Ektachrome. *4-color process*

46 Chemical painting. Exposed sheet of enlarging paper immersed briefly in stop bath, then painted with paper developer. After a short wait for the image to become strong, and the staining to reach desired level, the paper was fixed in usual method. *4-color process*

47 Colored light reflections. *4-color process*

48 Hypo crystals under white and colored lights. 4 x 5 Ektachrome. *4-color process*

49 Reflected colored lights. *4-color process*

50 Mortar and pestle. Colored lights and reflections. 35mm single-lens reflex. Kodachrome. *4-color process*

51-57 4 x 5 Ektachrome B. *4-color process*

58 4-color line separation of #54. In this reproduction the black printer has been omitted for special effects except in turret of microscope. *3-color process*

59-61 Infrared gas heat. Symbolic abstraction. Colored light sources and reflections. *4-color process*

62-65 4 x 5 Ektachrome B. *4-color process*

66-78 Assignment on water and air pollution. 35mm single-lens reflex. #70 and #72, High Speed Ektachrome. All others Kodachrome. *4-color process*

79-81 Pendulum light tracings. 2¼ x 2¼ twin-lens reflex. Ektachrome B. *4-color process*

82-85 Blood specimen slides. 35mm single-lens reflex. High Speed Ektachrome B. *4-color process*

86 Black and red line color transversion of black and white #147. *2-color line*

87 Color transversion of black and white #147. Arbitrary 4-color line separation printed in line. Kodalith. Ozachrome. *4-color line*

88 Continuous tone variation of #147. Stipple introduced in process. 4 x 5. Ektachrome. *4-color process*

Abstraction and Empathy
Wilhelm Worringer
New York: International Universities Press, Inc.

American Photographs
Walker Evans
The Museum of Modern Art, N. Y. Garden City, N. Y.: Doubleday & Company, Inc.

Anyone Can Paint
Arthur Zaidenberg
New York: Crown Publishers, Inc.

The Art of the Artist
Arthur Zaidenberg
New York: Crown Publishers, Inc.

The Art of Assemblage
William C. Seitz
The Museum of Modern Art, N. Y. Garden City, N. Y.: Doubleday & Company, Inc.

The Art of the Faker
Frank Arnav
Boston: Little, Brown & Company

Art Fakes & Forgeries
Fritz Mendax
London: Werner Laurie

Art Has Many Faces
Katherine Kuh
New York: Harper & Row, Publishers

Art and Illusion
(A. W. Mellon, E. H. Gombich Lectures)
New York: Pantheon Books for Bollingen Foundation

Art & Scholasticism
Jacques Maritain
New York: Charles Scribner's Sons

The Artist's Handbook of Materials and Techniques
Ralph Mayer
New York: The Viking Press

The Arts of Man
Eric Newton
Greenwich, Conn.: New York Graphic Society

Best of Art
Emily Genauer
Garden City, N. Y.: Doubleday & Company, Inc.

Changing Forms of Art
Patrick Heron
London: Routledge & Kegan Paul, Ltd.

A Color Notation
A. H. Munsell
Baltimore, Md.: Munsell Color Co., Inc.

Color Photography
Eliot Elisofon
New York: The Viking Press, Inc.

Concerning the Spiritual in Art
Wassily Kandinsky
New York: George Wittenborn Inc.

Creative Color
Faber Birren
New York: Reinhold Publishing Corporation

Creative Disciplines
Toska Tolces
Portland, Maine: The Bond Wheelwright Co.

The Creative Photographer
Andreas Feininger
Englewood Cliffs, N. J.: Prentice-Hall, Inc.

Creative 35mm Techniques
A. E. Woolley
New York: A. S. Barnes and Company, Inc.

The Decisive Moment
Henri Cartier-Bresson
New York: Simon and Schuster, Inc.

Design by Photography
O. R. Croy
London and New York: Focal Press

Designs in Nature
Tet Borsig
New York: The Viking Press, Inc.

Dictionary of Modern Painting
New York: Tudor Publishing Company

Dynamic Dissonance in Nature and the Arts
Louis Danz
New York: Farrar, Straus and Young

The Face of New York
Andreas Feininger
New York: Crown Publishers, Inc.

Flemish & Dutch Drawing
Colin T. Eisler
New York: Shorewood Publisher, Inc.

Form and Function
Horatio Greenough
Berkeley, California: University of California Press

The Form of Things Unknown
Herbert Read
New York: Horizon Press

Foundation of Modern Art
Ozenfant
New York: Dover Publications, Inc.

A Glossary of Art Terms
John O'Dwyer and Raymond Le Mage
New York: The Philosophical Library

Good and Bad Taste
Odd Brochmann
New York: The Macmillan Company

Great Moments in News Photography
John Faber
Toronto: Thomas Nelson & Sons

The Heaven of Invention
George Boas
Baltimore: Johns Hopkins Press

How to Understand Modern Art
George Flanagan
New York: The Studio Publications Inc.; Thomas Y. Crowell Co.

Ilford Manual of Photography
Ilford, Essex: Ilford Limited

International Photography Yearbook 1961
Norman Hall, editor
New York: St. Martin's Press

The Inward Vision
Paul Klee
New York: Harry N. Abrams, Inc.

Keys to Art
John Canaday
New York: Tudor Publishing Company

The Labyrinth
William Steinberg
New York: Harper & Row Publishers

Language of Vision
Gyorgy Kepes
Chicago: Paul Theobald

Learning to Look
Joshua C. Taylor
Chicago: The University of Chicago Press

A Life In Photography
Edward Steichen
Garden City, N. Y.: Doubleday & Company, Inc.

Living with a Camera
Alexander Spoerl
New York: Thomas Y. Crowell Co.

Looking into Art
Frank Seiberling
State University of Iowa
New York: Henry Holt and Co., Inc.

Marcel Duchamp
Robert Lebel
New York: Grove Press, Inc.

Masters of Photography
edited by Beaumont and Nancy Newhall
New York: Bonanza Books

Michelangelo's Theory of Art
Robert J. Clements
New York: New York University Press

Moments Preserved
Irving Penn
New York: Simon and Schuster, Inc.

The Naked Truth and Personal Vision
Barlett H. Hayes, Jr.
Addison Gallery of American Art, Andover, Mass.: Phillips Academy

Nature in Abstraction
John I. H. Baur
New York: The Macmillan Company

New Horizons in Color
Faber Birren
New York: Reinhold Publishing Corporation

The Origins of Art
Gene Weltfish
Indianapolis and New York: The Bobbs-Merrill Company, Inc.

Philosophies of Art & Beauty
Edited by Albert Hofstadter and Richard Kuhns
New York: The Modern Library, Inc.

Photo Maxima III
Hope Sanders
New York: Triton Press, Inc.

Pictures to Live With
compiled and edited by Bryan Holme
New York: The Viking Press, Inc.

Point and Line to Plane
Wassily Kandinsky
Bloomfield Hills, Michigan: Cranbrook Press

Museum without Walls
Andre Malraux
New York: The Bollingen Series, Pantheon Books

The Quiet Eye
Sylvia Shaw Judson
Chicago: Henry Regnery Company

The Reproduction of Colour
R. W. G. Hunt
Research Laboratories, Kodak Ltd. Harrow, London: Fountain Press

The Responsibility of the Artist
Jacques Maritain
New York: Charles Scribner's Sons

The Revolution of Color
Jean Gienier
New York: Tudor Publishing Company

Shooting an Elephant
George Orwell
New York: Harcourt, Brace & Co.

The Story of Modern Art
Sheldon Cheney
New York: The Viking Press, Inc.

Such, Such Were the Joys
George Orwell
New York: Harcourt, Brace & World, Inc.

Total Picture Control
Andreas Feininger
New York: Crown Publishers Inc.

The Twilight of the Absolute
Andre Malraux
New York: The Bollingen Series, Pantheon Books

Under the Sun
Nathan Lyons, Syl Labrot, Walter Chappell
New York: George Braziller, Inc.

U. S. Camera International Pictures 1963
Edited Tom Maloney
Associated Mary P. R. Thomas,
Jack L. Terracciano
Des Moines, Iowa: Duell, Sloan & Pearce

Vision & Design
Roger Fry
New York: Meridian Books

Vision in Motion
L. Moholy-Nagy
Chicago: Paul Theobald

The Visual Arts
Wallace S. Baldinger in collaboration with Harry B. Green
New York: Holt, Rinehart and Winston, Inc.

William Thon: The Painter and His Techniques
Alan D. Gruskin
New York: The Viking Press, Inc.

The World of Atget
Berenice Abbott
New York: Horizon Press

The World of Werner Bischof
Manuel Glasser
New York: E. P. Dutton & Co., Inc.

The World is Young
Wayne Miller
New York: Ridge Press, distributed by Simon and Schuster, Inc.

6203.